Confident Commercial Property Investment

A New Starter's Guide To Investing In Commercial Property

Natasha Collins

ISBN: 9781068777516 Paperback

Published by: Inspired By Publishing

Edited by: John Mansfield

The strategies in this book are presented primarily for enjoyment and educational purposes. Every effort has been made to trace copyright holders and obtain their permission for the use of copyright material.

The information and resources provided in this book are based upon the authors' personal experiences. Any outcome, income statements or other results, are based on the authors' experiences and there is no guarantee that your experience will be the same. There is an inherent risk in any business enterprise or activity and there is no guarantee that you will have similar results as the author as a result of reading this book.

The author reserves the right to make changes and assumes no responsibility or liability whatsoever on behalf of any purchaser or reader of these materials.

This book also comes with complimentary resources that support you in investing in commercial property. Get access to your resources here ncrealestate.co.uk/book

Acknowledgements

I wasn't sure that I would ever write a book on commercial property, mainly because I didn't want it to be boring and text book-y, and also because I really wasn't sure how I was going to put it together, but here it is. It was Steve Wallis who kept bringing it back up and telling me to write it; thank you for pushing me in the book writing direction. Thank you, Kathleen Vandervort for keeping me accountable with this book. From the time I started writing when we went to Chicago, you constantly asked me about it all the way through to publishing and made sure that I made this an actual thing—thank you for believing in me. Thank you to John Mansfield who took the time to go through and edit this book. You believed in the book and style of writing and have helped me make it even better than I thought it could be. Thank you so much to Argentina Leyva who took the most gorgeous cover photos for me. A big thank you to Chloë Bisson and the whole team at Inspired By Publishing for getting excited by the book and putting it out there.

I wouldn't have been able to do this without the incredible support from my family, team and friends. Chris Cairns (my wonderful husband) and Harry never doubt anything I do, and make sure I have the space to finish things whilst also lifting me up in the in-between moments. I love you both so much... Harry, this is your instruction manual for running the commercial part of the portfolio, I wrote it for you. Summer, obviously you get an honourable mention. Mum, Melanie Collins, you've always told me I should write a book; I'm not sure that this is the book you imagined, but you've always been the biggest fan of my career and my investment journey, and gave me the confidence to move forward and take a leap when things are feeling messy. You've been there with a glass of wine and a hug, you've never doubted anything I've suggested and instead have just been a constant support. Dad, thank you for letting me rant when things get tough, looking after everything that goes on in Bath and being the sounding board when I need a second opinion. Thank you Nicola Endacott for watching out for NCRE and picking up the slack when I've needed to put attention into this book (or anywhere else) and being the voice of reason at all times, and to Sam Coleman and Caroline Saxon for looking after our clients in the Members Club.

Honestly, I have the most amazing support and group of people around me: Amy Hobbs, Sophie Collins (my sisters who literally stick up for me no matter what), Laura Snell, Rach Cass, Kate Staiger, Amy Cheng and Stefan Ludlow thank you for never doubting that anything I say is possible, listening during times when I don't know how I'm going to get out of situations and believing that everything will work out. I love you all so much, I'm so proud that you're part of my circle. The women who have been with me along for the ride in this crazy property world — Ramina Jenkins, Bola Bakare, Pasq Puglisi, Nishita Gudka — honestly your pick me ups along the way and your advice, support and showing up for me and my business and life really means the world to me, I couldn't have got this far without you.

Thank you to my amazing clients for putting in the work, buying the properties and trusting me to be a part of your portfolio. I love working with you and problem solving with you. I can't wait to work with you to buy and manage more properties.

Finally, thank you for picking up this book and reading it. I hope it inspires you to dive further into your commercial property investment journey.

Contents

Introduction to Commercial Property Investment

I've always held the belief that commercial property is more lucrative than residential property. But, as with the majority of investors, I started out buying residential property. It was my easiest way into investment.

However, I had a different advantage in commercial property. I was managing large commercial and mixed-use property portfolios. I was training to be, and eventually qualified as, a commercial surveyor. My richest clients were the ones who held commercial property–residential was certainly flashier and certainly made an impact on their revenue stream. However, the bedrock that held the portfolio together was the commercial property with longer leases and larger rental incomes, which provided dependable quarterly income in substantial amounts. Plus, for the majority of leases there was the benefit that they were on full repairing and insuring terms, which meant that the tenants paid for absolutely everything: maintenance, utility bills, rebuilding insurance, business rates. Moreover, because commercial tenants were businesses, everything was done in a business relationship, it wasn't personal. I relished that. Tenants closing their doors at the end of business hours are not emailing or calling at night or at weekends or bank holidays (I can't guarantee this 100% of the time, sometimes I get out of hours calls). When it came to lease renewals, rent reviews or any other lease events, negotiations were dealt with in a (usually) professional manner and, for the most part, responses would follow some sort of rationale.

With all of that, I loved it. I liked the fact that you could alter the building value by negotiating on a lease or changing the rent around. I liked the spreadsheets that work behind the running of a building to make sure their value is maintained or increased and I liked that I could predict how the asset was going to perform, especially when I looked at the leases combined with the market.

Here's the other thing that I love: You can get into this market anywhere at a price point that works for you. Commercial properties are marketed based on their value. Granted, an agent will probably massage the asking price up somewhat, after all if you don't ask you don't get and it's hard to negotiate up after you've set the price. The broad principle is that the current rent or the potential rental income is either multiplied by the yield multiplier or divided by the yield to get to the value of the property.

Sounds like jargon?

Let's take a quick example. If the rental income on a property is £15,000 per annum and the appropriate and observed yield in the area is 8%, you would either do: 100 / 8 = 12.5 (12.5 is the yield multiplier, the rule is to divide 100 by the appropriate yield to get the multiplier) and then 12.5 x £15,000 = £187,500.

Alternatively, £15,000 / 0.08 (8% as a decimal) = £187,500.

£187,500 would be the rough value of the property.

This works in every location. If you have a low rental income, chances are that the property is going to be cheaper and vice versa. Alternately, if you have a higher yield, chances are the property is going to be cheaper than with a lower yield, where the property is going to be more expensive.

At this point, let me pause because I've probably blown your brain if you haven't come across this before. And that's OK. Yield is a measure of risk. If the yield is higher, it means there is more risk and therefore the value of the property will be lower. If the yield is lower than the risk is lower and the value of the property will be higher.

This will all become clearer the further we dive into this book. I wanted to reiterate the point that you could find different priced commercial property in all locations.

There isn't the North-South divide that residential investors tend to talk about.

Hopefully, I've piqued your interest slightly more. To recap, commercial property is more a numbers and spreadsheets game, with value being created in leasing strategies. Also, you can set your purchase price and buy almost anywhere, as it's all about rent and yield.

Sounds interesting, right? This is why commercial property is a great investment class to invest in.

You'll also note that the commercial property market goes in cycles. You've probably heard of the dying high street? It makes national news most weeks at the time of writing. The reason for this is that commercial property trends change, roughly every 5 years. This is because leases tend to last 5 years and obsolete businesses fall away, while stable or new innovative businesses take the lead. This may mean that certain types of buildings aren't needed as much. Currently, this is true of those large retail properties, for example the type that Debenhams used to occupy. This is normal. Trends change. Look at what you like now compared to 5, 10, 15 years ago.

You've changed too. The flavour of the month will be more profitable and those buildings that aren't in vogue won't be as profitable.

Expect this to happen—that's commercial property. The way you combat it isn't by getting upset that no one wants your building. It's to be innovative with your building. Change it into something that tenants do want or, even better, let tenants come in and be creative with it.

One thing I do know for sure is that commercial investors need to be resilient and they need to be prepared to get creative, think smart and not be beaten. You have to ride the wave in the good times, whilst saving for the bad times. You have to be the sort of thought leader that's prepared to make everything good again—or hire someone like me, an Asset Manager, to do that innovative thinking for you.

If that sounds like something you want to get your teeth into, I'm sure you and I are going to enjoy this voyage into commercial property together. After all, the most success comes to those who are constantly thinking forward, not staying stuck in the past.

The Takeaway

1. Commercial property offers real alternatives to residential investment in the medium and long-term.
2. Commercial property offers a different management approach due to the relationship between landlord and tenant.
3. Commercial property provides scope for creative use by the landlord to optimise income.
4. Commercial property's value is based on its rental income and the yield observed in the marketplace.

1

Types of Commercial Property

When I'm talking about commercial property I'm mainly talking about retail and office space. The term 'Commercial Multiple Occupancy (CMO)' is being used a lot and is used where there are multiple commercial tenants in one building.

Let's start though with a brief discussion on industrial, otherwise known as sheds. Industrial is in its prime right now. With retail habits changing, more and more people are choosing to shop online. That means there is more need for storage rather than shopfronts (think about the Amazon model). With this demand, rent has soared and yields have come down which means that this type of property has increased in value over the years. This can be seen as a good thing. The continuing demand means that the property will always be let.

With industrial you do need to make sure it is right for the right tenant. If you want to simply let the unit as storage you need to make sure the property is water tight and secure and that it's not going to burn down. If you want to let it for retailing purposes, it needs to be a little bit more high spec. Good access for delivery lorries is mandatory, so look at the roads into the unit and whether the necessary vehicles can get in and out and turn around. You also need to make sure you have good size roller shutters or entrance into the unit. Then you need to think about location overall. Are you on a transport artery? Which areas of the country could the location serve? Would anyone want to have a hub here? Finally, you can then think about add-ons to the property. Could you add electric car charging? Or have other tenants in the parking area such as mobile food outlets? Be innovative–you'll have a lot of space when you buy this type of property so use it well.

Industrial Property Terminology

Light Industrial Property: Less than 10,000 sq. ft. and buildings which include a dock or roll-up door (similar to a garage)

Industrial Property: Broadly encompasses all types of property which is used for the manufacturing or storage of goods

Specialised Industrial Property: Warehouses that are used by tenants with special needs, for example, cold storage or a data hub.

Let's turn to retail. The face of the retail market is changing. Online shopping has drastically changed the way that retailers position themselves. It's definitely cheaper for them to be online and simply trade from the shop face of their website, with a storage unit in a cheaper location (nudge nudge, industrial owners–this is where you should be cashing in). Despite the changes, it definitely does not mean that the High Street is dead. Firstly, it's important for retailers to keep a presence, somewhere they can catch footfall. If it's in a prime spot, then usually this will be more of a flagship store, where they brand it and make it a destination. A prime retail location would be Oxford Street and Bond Street in London or the best shopping destination in other cities or towns. Secondary retail locations are usually more where it's at. These are streets adjacent to the prime streets. The premises are cheaper, so the retailer can get more bang for their buck, but then the downside is that they have to put more effort into getting the customer to walk into their shop. Don't be deterred though, often retailers will follow one another, so chances are that a secondary space could become prime as the shopping street moves to a more cost-effective destination (luckily for you, you get to cash-in on the market uplift at rent review).

Prime Property Investments

In this chapter, I have explained about prime locations for retail. Don't get this confused with Prime Investment Assets which refers to properties that provide a combination of stores and amenities tailored to suit the preferences and needs of the local population.

Another important aspect of retail property is that the units are measured differently. The units are given a measurement In Terms of Zone A (ITZA). The unit is divided into zones starting at the shop front, usually each zone is 6.096m in depth. The first 6.096m deep zone at the shop front is referred to as Zone A, the next 6.096m depth is Zone B and so on. Zone A is the most valuable area of the shop and is value weighted at 1. Zone B is value weighted at 0.5, and then you half-back each of the other zones. Generally, Zones end at D or E (depending on the depth of the unit) with the rest of the space considered as 'remainder'. Basements, upper floors, kitchens, offices or any other ancillary space are put into different Zones and given an appropriate value. That's the general rule of thumb, anyway. If you are in super-prime retail areas, like Oxford Street or Regent Street, then the Zones are deeper and differing zoning principles are adopted in different areas. I've learnt throughout the years that there doesn't seem to be a hard and fast rule from Zone C onwards, so it's up for negotiation. But those are the principles. You can use comparable evidence to get the ITZA rental ($£/m^2$) and then multiply it to the calculated Zone depths to calculate the market rent for the unit.

Example:

Zone	Area – M²	Multiplier	Area ITZA
A	30	1	30
B	32	0.5	16
C	28	0.25	7
Kitchen	10	0.1	1
		Total	54
		Market ITZA Rent	£100/m2
		Total Rent Per Year for Unit	£5,400 per annum

It's best to get a surveyor who specialises in lease advisory to negotiate on rent, as they are worth their money and will be able to get all of the evidence you need to successfully negotiate a good deal.

You could also fill your retail unit with a restaurant. Such space can be very popular with restaurateurs who are looking for a quirky space to install their fabulous food creations. Restaurant operators rarely want prime space, but you need to make sure that there is room for kitchens and ample space for dining.

Restaurants are measured as a whole. The ground floor is usually given a 1 weighting with basements and kitchens zoned at 0.5. These multipliers are then applied to the measured floor areas before calculating the market rent for the unit using ITZA rental evidence.

One of my biggest tips for retail units is to buy a unit that is in demand. I would start looking around at gaps in the local market for a certain type of retailer or restaurant. Then use sources such as Estates Gazette or Loop Net to find out what spaces those types of tenants are on the lookout for. You can even phone the estates or acquisitions departments for any brands that you identify as missing from an area and see if they would be interested in taking a unit. If you can find somewhere that fits the bill then it's worthwhile trying to organise a deal. What you don't want to do is buy a retail unit and have it sit empty - the longer it is empty, the less likely you are to find tenants. The unfortunate reality is that tenants are not attracted to units that look like they won't get custom. They want buzzy, lively places with people walking past, easy transport links, a good tenant mix of retailers and restaurants, limited competition and somewhere they can imagine establishing themselves. So, you have to give them that dream, even if that's simply filling the space with a pop-up tenant, or something interesting whilst you wait to fill it. Be that space that tenants dream of and be that person who makes it easy for them to get what they want.

Offices are slightly different to retail, although what you will usually find is that you will get office space on top of a retail unit in a block. That's not a bad thing, as it's good to diversify your properties with different tenant mixes, and you can always ask the retailer if they want an additional office if you run out of anywhere else to ask (although if you buy right, that won't be a necessity).

With office space, you want to make sure that you are in close proximity to transport and, where necessary, have availability for staff to park cars. Office blocks also need to have good facilities, toilets, kitchens and lifts (where possible). However, as per one of the awesome perks of office space, your tenants will contribute to the cost of running all of this via the service charge, which means it's cheaper for you to run.

The other thing to remember about office space is that the tenants aren't looking to attract footfall, they are just looking for a space that works for their team. You need to understand where the demand is in the market for office space and provide it.

A huge boom in the office industry is the rise of serviced office space and I'm a massive fan of this. It is flexible, allows for co-working and businesses can have as much or as little of space as they want. Also, the rent is all-inclusive, meaning that the service charge, utilities and rates are all packaged into one monthly fee. It's very similar to residential serviced accommodation, such as Airbnb.

When you're pricing service office space you need to think about all the costs associated with running the building as that's going to come out of your pocket rather than the tenants. Based on an average cost of running buildings, the expenditure I budget for is around £4/ft^2 (£40/m^2) per annum. These budget figures were being used at the time of writing. You will need to adapt them to your building. These figures are useful for a first check to see if the deal stacks, or could potentially stack. If you decide to proceed with the deal you can then take this one step further and get more detailed and accurate costs.

I suggest if you are buying a building that you are going to use as a serviced office building on your first viewing, take all of the metre readings and then go and inspect again and take another round of metre reads and calculate how much the utility expenditure will be. You can also then speak to the current owner and see if they have any accounts with expenditure that they can share.

When we're thinking of a serviced office space plan for 150 sq. ft. for every 2 people in an office, you can then split your building out accordingly. You may want to provide a mixture of larger and smaller spaces.

You also may see one space let to multiple people. For example, in a hairdresser's, each of the individual chairs may be let as opposed to the unit as a whole. In one unit, an owner was letting shelving space at £15/shelf per month to different artists. Here you can price accordingly depending on demand. However, if you aren't giving exclusive occupation of a space to one individual then you will need to offer a licence rather than a lease. Licences are significantly less valuable than leases when it comes to valuing a property. More on this later.

If this seems like too much hassle, yet you think your space would be a perfect fit for this type of use, then you could always approach one of the larger serviced office space providers and see if they will rent your space from you. And then in turn, sublet it on a shared office space basis. Do your research here first, as you will need to pitch it to these providers so that they come and take a look. You can go and explore serviced office spaces simply by booking a visit to have a wander around. Market research is key here.

Usually, once you've filled your office space and you are providing your tenants with a really good place to base themselves, unless the business has a massive growth spurt, chances are they will want to stay. So capitalise on that–it will be lucrative for you.

One change to the market, which has been especially great for Landlords, is the introduction of Use Class E. This Use Class encompasses retail, office, cafes, restaurants, GP surgeries, light industrial, creches, gyms and more, opening up spaces to a variety of users. This means that when your unit becomes vacant there are more options for tenants. Use this to your advantage, as this opens you up to a whole new possibility of how tenants use space. Allow this to happen rather than be restrictive. Innovative tenants create profitable businesses.

That's a broad overview of the different types of commercial property. Yes, if you look at the Town and Country Planning (Use Classes) Order 1987 (as amended), you will find a wider range of commercial property types, such as leisure, hotels and supported living. These are more specialised but in this book, I am focusing on industrial, retail and office property.

The Takeaway

1. 'Commercial' describes a large property sector within which a wide range of money-making activity is carried out by tenants–retail, office, leisure, industrial. These sectors can be segmented further.

2. Commercial locations can be differentiated into prime, secondary and tertiary.

3. Commercial occupiers have different needs and requirements from the property they occupy.

4. Different commercial property types are measured and valued using different approaches.

2

Advantages and Disadvantages of Commercial Property Investment

Before jumping on the commercial property investment bandwagon, it's really important that you are as informed as possible about what you are buying into. I like to go through this with a SWOT analysis and look at the strengths, weaknesses, opportunities and threats of an investment type.

<u>Strengths</u>

The strengths of commercial property are that commercial leases are for longer periods so you don't have to be looking for new tenants as often. Leases typically are for 5 years, although they could be shorter, around 3 years or stretch out to 10 years.

Leases are also much more landlord- (and arguably tenant-) friendly. The lease is agreed by both parties when the tenant is interested in taking the space and usually all the lease terms are open to negotiation so that both parties know exactly what they are taking on. It's transparent. Leases are explicit about which party is responsible for what and should be your guide to that landlord and tenant relationship. Leases also provide for forfeiture which means that if you no longer want the lease in place and if the tenant fails to pay the rent, you can go in and forfeit the lease without the need to go through the courts.

Commercial leases also expressly state who is responsible for maintenance within the building. Usually all of the repair, maintenance and decoration responsibilities will fall to the tenant, meaning less expenditure for the landlord. Similarly, the tenant will also pay for other outgoings such as full rebuilding insurance and business rates, so essentially the landlord will only have to pick up the costs for any lending and property management services.

Commercial tenants are businesses and this means firstly that any communication or negotiations aren't personal, so no hard feelings. Secondly, as they are businesses they open during business hours and are pretty self-sustainable. You're not going to get any of those late-night phone calls about a broken washing machine.

Commercial property investments are typically long-term investments, although the target should be that it completely repays your investment within 10-15 years, which is doable. At that point you will have been through the whole cycle with the property and can choose to keep it or sell it. When I talk about cycles in commercial property, I typically expect a property to move in a 5-10 year cycle depending on the leases. Within this time you will either have a few lease renewals or relettings and you will have had a chance to maintain or improve the property. Always think about commercial property as a minimum of a 10-year hold and see what it looks like over that period.

If you are investing in your SSAS, commercial property is a bread and butter asset that can provide good returns along with your other assets, and there are ways of structuring a deal so that you can get access to cash now and in your pension. Investing in commercial property using your Small Self Administered Scheme (SSAS) pension is also very tax efficient.

Weaknesses

With all investments there is of course going to be weaknesses and commercial property has them.

You will need to have more money to buy commercial property. If you are purchasing with financing you can expect to get a maximum loan to value of 70%, although at the time of writing it is usual for banks to only offer a 65% loan to value if you are buying in your SSAS.

A note on SSAS lending: your SSAS can borrow up to 50% of the total SSAS value, however some administrators limit you to 50% of the property value.

Commercial lending is also a tough market right now. It is really bank and property dependent, and you should expect high interest rates. At the time of writing, interest rates are between 6.8-9%. That's a huge swing. I would be expecting around 8%.

Market Value
The estimated amount for which an asset or liability should exchange on the valuation date between a willing buyer and a willing seller in an arm's length transaction, after proper marketing and where the parties had each acted knowledgeably, prudently and without compulsion (RICS, 2022).

Lenders are also tending to lend on Vacant Possession Value rather than Market Value on the property, even if there are tenants in the building paying rent. This is because they don't want to take on any risk with the property and therefore, if they do have to repossess the property and the tenants leave, then they should recoup all of their funds back. Vacant Possession Value can be 10-20% less than market value. An even bigger difficulty here is that Market Value will normally be the price you have agreed to pay for the property as that's the amount you've agreed to pay on the open market. Therefore, you'll have to make up the difference in cash, between the Market Value of the property and the Vacant Possession Value...unless you can negotiate downwards.

Other quirks lenders might ask for is for all of the commercial leases to run for more than 2 or more years with no breaks. This is a tough requirement to meet as many leases will have breaks. Lenders can ask for all full repairing and insuring leases, or certain tenant types. If you do get these funny requests, shop around for another deal. Whilst lenders are being tougher on their requirements, if you have a good deal there will be a lender who will work with you.

As a general rule it can take a while to let commercial property. Forecast for 6-9 months as minimum and then it is usual to offer a rent-free period for the tenant to come in and fit out the unit to their taste. Again, this is standard, but can be a big hit for the landlord who may have to pay for mortgage finance, business rates and contribute towards the service charges if there is no rental income coming in.

If you buy a property where there aren't any service charges in place to tenants or they aren't used to paying for their own maintenance and repairs, expect push back when you put this in place. This can be tough for new Landlords who aren't used to the process. Negotiations can be lengthy on this, but trust me, once all tenants are on board, the savings are huge. Short-term pain for long-term gain with this one. In the interim, whilst getting service charges in place, you will need to pick up all of the maintenance costs which can get expensive.

In October 2022, NC Real Estate acquired a retail arcade in Oxfordshire for one of our clients. At the time all tenants were on licences and the landlord paid for everything apart from electricity bills. The landlord started negotiations to introduce a service charge to the existing tenants. It took 4 months of negotiations to agree on a £2 per square foot service charge and in the meantime, the landlord picked up around £30,000 worth of costs to make sure that the tenants wouldn't be overly charged when the service charge kicked in. The landlord was generous here in doing the work, it could also have been an opportunity to patch and then put works through the service charge. However to get the tenants to agree there was a lot of good will from our client. In contrast, in another building NC Real Estate purchased in Cornwall, the client waited to do a lot of work until the service charge was in place. The building was purchased in December 2021, the new service charge started in July 2022. The tenants held off on paying until September because they didn't want to stomach the costs of £3 per square foot even though there were service charge clauses baked into their leases, which my client inherited. As the previous landlord had never charged service charges, the tenants didn't see why they had to pay service charges now.

I've listed this as a weakness because as the landlord you have to have patience and understanding. You might have to stump up some cash to do maintenance, repair and decoration while the service charge budget is agreed and implemented with the tenants. As you'll see in both of those case studies, the service charge budgets are in, so it ended up being a massive win, but it took time. You have to make sure that the tenants understand that the service charge is for the benefit of the building, not for the landlord.

Which brings me to another note: If a lease has a service charge clause in it, charge it. No excuses. You aren't being nice to a tenant by charging *ad hoc*, instead give them something to budget for.

Opportunities

With all investments there are opportunities and this is especially true with commercial property investment.

I want to make it clear again, if you are an innovative thinker and push the bounds of what is normal chances are you'll find opportunities.

On my podcast I'd been threatening for a while that I was going to buy a telephone box. I'm not the sort of person who says something and doesn't follow through. However at the start of 2022 I didn't have a spare £10k+ to put towards this type of purchase. Fast forward 6 months, I had some business profits that I needed to find a home for and so transferred £15k into my SSAS pension.

At the same time, I'd been watching the telephone box auctions on BidX and had seen a number of telephone boxes in London go up for sale. I emailed the agent and said I had roughly £10k to spend on a telephone box–did he have anything? The answer was yes-ish if I was prepared to pay £11,200, but it was on a side street with not much pedestrian access. I didn't mind, it was 3ft x 3ft in London. 'Yes please!' I said, 'Send me the contracts.' Well, I was sent a contract for a telephone box at 148-150 Southampton Row (Russell Square!!) for £11,200... This was being marketed for £15k! I jumped at it, signed the contracts and then with the signed contract email, I also said 'Are you sure? This wasn't the one I was expecting.' They replied, 'You've signed the contract now.' Woohoo, I was the proud owner of a telephone box full of rubbish. I cleaned it out, put retail stands in there, fixed the windows and put advertising vinyl inside. The total cost for the purchase price, agency fees and making it into a retail unit: £15,169.44. Currently, it lets out for £80 per month as advertising space. However, as I'm writing this, an agent has approached me to advise that they can let it for £1,500 per year. Details to follow. If you're in London, go to 148-150 Southampton Row and take a look at what it's doing (mine's the one with the lockbox on the bottom).

I spotted an opportunity and rather than thinking, 'What if this doesn't work?!' I thought, 'Hell yes, I'm going to make it work!'

There are opportunities in commercial property everywhere and therefore, I'd always start by looking at opportunities within your search area or close to home. Start with the macros, look at local developments for housing, infrastructure, utilities, schools, transport, improvements, town plans and commercial tenants who've announced they are moving to the area. If this shows signs of life in an area, it means there is a chance to capitalise on an improving location.

Then drill down: What commercial property is available to buy? What tenants would take that space if it's empty? Assess the lease, can you renegotiate new terms soon or increase the rent?

I never see any of these things as a negative until I've assessed the market. As long as the commercial property is in a good location with demand then there will be tenants who want it. So, adopting that mindset, your due diligence will be based around how you can push the market to make your building generate more income.

Going back to the Oxfordshire case study I discussed earlier, when I assessed the building with my client, we identified these opportunities:

- There is a vacant space to let which means that there's an opportunity to increase the income which will up the value.
- Tenants seem willing to agree to new leases which means you get security of rental.
- Long-term you can put in place rent increases as the market improves which means you will always be growing your income from this property.
- Lidl is moving into the area as it believes there is an appropriately-sized customer base there which is a good sign of growth in the area.

These opportunities panned out and more. The vacant unit was let in month one to a massage therapist who loved the space–and at a new record rent of £28.50 per square foot (up from around £18 per square foot).

The tenants agreed to new 5-year leases (a departure from their rolling 1-month licences) with break clauses at either year 2 or year 3, which gave the landlord more security knowing that the rent would be coming in for longer. All the rents went up in line with the new letting. To phase this in gently for the older tenants, stepped rents were introduced which averaged out over a 5 year period to the higher rent increase.

Finally, and the best opportunity that came from this, a neighbouring landlord sold his two retail units off market, at a discount to my client as he saw what my client was doing and didn't have the wherewithal to do it himself and needed the money.

You don't always know what the knock-on opportunity will be when you buy, but again I stress, if you can see a property being perfect for a certain type of tenant or you can imagine a fabulous space, then aim for that reality.

Threats

Threats are also another part of investing. There is always going to be something hovering just out of view which might, and I repeat *might*, make the investment lose value.

One of the big things that threaten commercial landlords at the moment is energy performance. The Department for Business, Energy and Business Strategy (2021) consulted on whether commercial EPC's should have a mandatory C rating by 2027 and a mandatory B rating by 2030 (Energy Advice Hub, (2023). At the time of writing this isn't legislation yet, instead as of the 1st April 2023 all buildings must have a minimum energy efficiency rating of an E (GOV.UK, 2023). But the Government are very keen on sustainability and the likelihood is that they will look to improve of minimum energy efficiency standards when you let or own a commercial property.

Yes, this will mean expenditure on your building, unless you can get an exemption (the reference for GOV.UK,

2023 has a link to the website where you can find the exemption).

You can also turn this into a great thing. Tenants love a sustainable building, it costs them less to run and so they don't have to factor in for huge energy bills. That saving means that they will pay a premium on rent. Therefore, it is a good idea to look at the EPC for your building and the recommendations report and investigate what you can do to make the EPC better. Cost it up and then do a feasibility study on the difference between implementing the recommendations, the energy saving and how much more you can charge on rent, and I think you'll be surprised what small tweaks do to the building.

The next threat is the Base Rate rises.

If we go back to what I said at the start about valuing commercial property rental, income is multiplied by yield. Yield is a measure of risk. The lower the yield, the higher the value of a property; the higher the yield, the lower the value of a property. The yield of a commercial property should never be lower than the Base Rate. Therefore, as the Base Rate rises all commercial property prices should rise with it, which means that the value of your commercial property should decrease.

That's OK. Commercial property values do increase and decrease cyclically anyway. However, you need to be aware of this change and watch the macro-economic indicators for potential future changes so that you can predict how the value of your property will change. Yields aren't everything in value, the stability and longevity of your rent are also a key indicator, so a movement in yields isn't going to change everything, though again I stress—it *will* have some impact.

Changes in the Base Rate will also mean that lending and finance will get more expensive. This is a threat because it will mean, if you are relying on finance, that interest costs may increase and you won't be bringing in as much income. Again, there are ways of mitigating this, such as paying down on your mortgages or improving the quality of your investment. For example, if you can put longer leases in place with good security (for example via a large rental deposit or a guarantor) and a strong covenant tenant that has sound financial backing, you are more likely to be offered lower interest rates.

Base Rate changes are a result of inflation. Inflation causes costs to skyrocket and this can impact a tenant's ability to pay rent or other outgoings on a property. This is a big threat as it can stop a tenant from being able to pay rent and service charge in a timely manner. This threat can only be managed by speaking to the tenant, so don't assume that you know their situation. If you've spoken to them and they say they're OK, believe them. If they say they need help, offer a payment plan or a rent concession. Ultimately agree to something that's mutually beneficial. Communication is key.

Threats are also changing demands for space and areas. Gentrification or redevelopment of an area can make it look new, flashy and the place that everyone, including tenants, want to be. This can take demand and footfall away from other areas which traditionally were buoyant markets and make them ghost towns. This doesn't happen overnight, but slowly migration happens. It's the cycle of towns and cities and eventually, one day, the development comes back around.

Knowing that information, that change is inevitable, you want to be strategic.

Firstly, your due diligence is key. Take a look at areas that are being redeveloped. That area is going to be the *creme de la creme* of places to be, so think about how you can find a property that benefits from that new development but is also connected to other local areas too, so that not all of your eggs are in the brand shiny new basket, but instead gets the footfall and customers from that area by being on a transport route. Secondly, I want you to think about this, because I do all the time. One of the wisest things I ever heard a property professional say was from Maureen Ehrenberg at the World Built Environment Forum in New York in 2019. At the time Maureen was the Global Head of Digital Facility and Asset Management Services at WeWork (yes, I know what happened to WeWork, they didn't fail because of their property team, they failed because they overspent on ridiculous things so hear me out) and her advice on buying and fitting-out buildings was to make the shell stable, but allow the insides to be adaptable as commercial trends change every 5 years. Your building should be able to adapt to that. I agree. If you can be adaptable, threats from a changing local area won't hit you as hard, or even at all, because you will be able to adapt.

Remember, all you've got to do is buy a building that tenants will want to operate from, so demand is key. Keep reshaping your building to achieve demand.

The Takeaway

1. Commercial property ownership provides a range of advantages.
2. A detailed SWOT analysis of a property type or a location is beneficial in gaining a better understanding of the opportunities it can bring you.
3. Adaptability in use, space design and letting strategy will help improve income stream over time.
4. You owe it to yourself to ensure that due diligence is undertaken before lasting decisions are made.

3

Your Goals

I get it, you are reading this book because you want to make money in commercial property. It's what everybody tells me. Then they proceed to tell me the number of properties that they want to buy, in the hope that I'm going to go, 'Aha, yup, I know exactly what you want.' The problem with just plucking a random number of properties out of the air is that 1) It has no meaning and 2) You've given me such a ridiculous figure which even you don't believe. So I'll tell you this, you aren't going to get to where you want to be.

I've only once been given the perfect answer from the get-go. It was amazing to read this client's goals bio. They had gone into depth about what they wanted to achieve each month from the start, up to their 10-year plan. They had even been so detailed to put in time for learning, making mistakes and realistic income goals. Yet, they also weren't afraid to dream big. Goals of luxury beach retreats, days sat on the sand contemplating the crystal-clear blue water. This clarity, doesn't only gives this client the drive to keep persisting no matter what, it also gives them room for error. They get to forgive themselves, so the pressure is off. There is just an unwavering belief that they will get to where they need to be. Trust me here, they definitely will, I also hold that unwavering belief for them.

It's the detail of your goals that will keep you focused.

I'm going to get you to work with me now to set your goals and your intentions for your property journey. No matter where you are right now, let's stop and get this chapter sorted, because everything else that comes later, you will be able to handle.

To start with, I want you to fast forward to your future, that point where you've built a commercial property portfolio.

What does this look like to you? What is the property portfolio providing for you? How much time are you spending working on it, or have you handed everything over to an asset manager or property manager?

When I started visualising what I wanted to be, I couldn't imagine it. I stumbled and started, looking for the picture of my best self. It turned out that what I craved most was the freedom to choose my location—travelling and working while earning a reliable income—so I could spend my time more freely. I love working, I love a new challenge so NC Real Estate fulfils that. I also have an income from my property portfolio…tick.

I now want you to consider your money situation. What is it that you need from property? I'm not talking about what you want here, I'm simply talking about what you need down to the penny. Get that spreadsheet out and start calculating. Mortgage, bills, gym, child care, car, pets, other hobbies, food shopping, eating out, other shopping, extra money left over. Whatever the figure is, just acknowledge it, that's what you are going to aim for.

Disclaimer: This exercise could take a while as it can be super hard to eye up your expenses. But be brave here. The knowledge of your outgoings will drive you to create that income.

Investing in property might not be for the income. If this is you, that's OK too. What do you want it to fund? Building up your pension so you can keep investing? Your children's school fees? Describe that.

I now want you to consider why. Why do you want to do this, why is it important to you to invest in property? Is it for yourself, your family? Do you just want a challenge and this seems like the best opportunity you've got? I want your why, why, whys.

Get specific, get tough and get passionate. You are doing this for a reason. Why are you doing it?

One of the scariest things my Dad ever said to me was, 'Your generation will never retire, let alone get a pension.' Urgh, how terrifying is that! I'd grown up seeing my grandparents retire quite comfortably. It seemed like the norm: Grow up, get old, retire at 65, chill out and then be the life and soul of the party throughout your elder years. Yet, my Dad's speech haunted me. So I decided to make a change to my life so that I could always have the time and money I need whilst exploring the world, loving my awesome family and giving the best I possibly could to everyone. The decision was property, I was going to make it through property and so I began. And haven't looked back since.

Back to your whys. Are you clearer now, what you are doing this for? Does it make sense to you?

Write it all down. It's exciting, right?

Let's bring this fabulous stuff down a peg or two. I now want you to analyse where you are right now. What is it that's going on in your life? Just be totally honest. What is true for you right now? It could be what you work for, your living situation, your income situation. Get it out. What is happening today?

The reason that I want you to do this is because today is where it all begins, where your property journey starts. There is absolutely no judgement about how much you know, how many properties you've got, or your current circumstance. I just want you to keep a note of exactly where you are.

If you've got a piece of paper in front of you with all of your goals, I want you to write down on the other side of the paper where you are today. I then want you to join up the two sides with an arrow pointing towards your goals. It's that arrow we are crossing here! It doesn't look so scary mapping it out in this way does it? A simple arrow to walk along on the way to your goals. It's completely doable!

For an informational book, all of that goals stuff is rather out there. However, throughout my life the pattern of success follows what I write down. I'm sure you've heard the saying 'what you focus on grows.' I firmly believe it.

The steps to property investment are simple. The process isn't easy. You are going to will yourself through a lot of it, because you can get impatient when it's slow. Frustrated when things don't go your way. Property investment is full of highs and lows, which is why every single time you lose focus, I want you to pick up your goals map and remind yourself of why you are doing this.

Your goals are your motivation, they need to make you stay the path so make them strong enough that, no matter how painful it is, you'll keep going.

It's time to become that successful property investor you are so destined to be!

Before I wrap up this chapter, I want to walk you through my goals and my property portfolio. To be clear, I don't feel that it's necessary to share the ins and outs of your portfolio with anyone, but I also understand that your imposter syndrome can jump out when you see that other people may have better portfolios than you, in which case it makes you feel shame or guilt that you haven't achieved enough.

When I run Facebook Ads, this is the trolling that I get: allegedly I haven't achieved enough to be an expert in commercial property. After all, said troll has Googled me and found my 5 companies, two of which are dissolved because I don't use them, one company *only* has two commercial properties in there, one company is my firm of surveyors and the final one is an old company which I use to lend money in and out of.

What are they expecting at this point? For me to think, 'Oh yes, you got me, sorry I'm not good enough because I don't meet whatever criteria you think describes success'?

Of course I'm not doing that. I stay in my lane. Plus, what a troll thinks of me is none of my business.

I'm a qualified chartered surveyor, with years of professional experience *and* teaching experience. I know my stuff because I work in it day in and day out. It doesn't mean I have to own every single commercial property. After all, male gynaecologists aren't required to have female genitals in order to be considered highly experienced at their job.

I'll share my property portfolio with you. I believe in quality over quantity, and you should, too.

As of May 2024, I have three commercial units in the UK, three residential units in the UK and two residential units in the USA. I am very rarely in a single country to be able to focus a huge amount of attention on my portfolio. After all, I'm paid to build my clients' portfolios and that's where I focus.

The goal of my property portfolio is to give me something to retire on. I've been building my portfolio since 2011.

I purchased all my properties combined for £1,505,000 and today they are worth a combined £2,335,000, so I've made £830,000 in 13 years. The gross rental income for last year was £137,000 and the net rental income for last year was £40,500 as I did maintenance on two of the residential units in the UK.

Note: I didn't add my telephone box into this or anything that's in my SSAS pension. I see that as a completely different entity.

Do I need to add more to my portfolio? Not necessarily. Instead I'll focus on reducing costs because my net profit will go up. I can't say definitely that my goals won't change, but for now I'm earning more than the average UK salary and I have a business outside of this which I love to run.

Also, you've probably just looked at that and gone, '*Oh my goodness Natasha what a small portfolio!*' Yes, and?

I go back to my point, I really don't care what other people's portfolios look like as long as mine is working for me. It's bringing in an additional income and it's easy to run.

Everyone's goals are different, which is perfect because everyone is individual, which is why no two property portfolios should look the same.

The lesson here? Build a property portfolio which suits you and only you and your goals. Nothing else matters.

The Takeaway

1. Establish your investment goals and place them in a realistic time-frame.

2. A detailed and honest personal financial appraisal can help you assess if your goals can be achieved within your realistic time-frame.

3. The appraisal process will enable you to highlight the strengths in your ambition and to identify where you may need to adjust it.

4

Commercial Property Goals

Now that you've looked at your goals and what you would like to achieve as a general overall, let's get specific so that you know what you should be researching or searching for when you get to that place.

Here's the process.

Decide on how much cash you have available to spend on commercial property investment.

This could be the cash in your bank, the cash you're going to get from a remortgage, the amount in your SSAS pension, or the money you are getting from investors.

What is that total cash or money? Write it down here:

£_____

Decide on the Loan to Value (LTV) you want to have on average across your commercial property portfolio (If you are using your SSAS pension, this should be 50% LTV).

Loan to Value: _____

Then you need to decide on the gross yield you want to achieve. This is completely up to you. The maximum I would suggest in commercial property is 12%. Those types of properties are going to be harder to come by than those at 8%, so just remember that.

Gross Yield: _____

Your next step is to calculate your target overall portfolio purchase price.

To do this you need to do the following steps:

Step 1: 100% - your ideal LTV % = deposit as a %

Step 2: Total Cash / deposit as a % = Gross purchase price

Step 3: Gross purchase price * 6% = Purchasing costs

Step 4: Gross purchase price - Purchasing costs = Target overall portfolio purchase price

For example: say you had £100,000 in cash and you wanted the LTV to be 60%. The calculation would be as follows:

Step 1: 100% - 60% = 40%

Step 2: £100,000 / 40% = £250,000

Step 3: £250,000 * 0.06 (6% as a decimal) = £15,000

Step 4: £250,000 - £15,000 = £235,000

In this calculation it is expecting the purchasing costs to be 6%. This is slightly above average, but means you've got money in the bank for legal fees, Stamp Duty Land Tax and any other fees associated with lending.

You then need to calculate how much of a rental income you need.

This is a simple sum, which is your Target Overall Portfolio Purchase price multiplied by your ideal gross yield.

So, if my target gross yield was 9%, then the calculation would look like this:

Step 5: £235,000 * 0.09 (9% as a decimal) = Total rental income needed of £21,150 per annum.

Once you've got your Target Overall Portfolio Purchase price and the total rental income needed, you now have specific goals that you can go out and search for.

If my goal was a purchase price of £235,000 and a rental income of £21,150 per annum, chances are I could find that in one property.

However, if I multiplied that goal by 10, I could split that down into as many properties as I wanted to buy. I could, for example, target 7 properties at a purchase price of £335,000 with an income of £30,000 per annum. Or I could mix it up any which way I wanted to get to my overall goal.

It will be your property portfolio, choose what you want it to look like. Having this information means you've got a shopping list of exactly what you need and what you want to go out to the market to find.

Now, I know that there are some of you reading this who are going to be targeting return on capital employed (ROCE) as many investors do. This is essentially, the amount of capital in, versus the amount of capital out after the first remortgage, or sale. The spreadsheet you can download will do this for you.

Often this figure can get in the way of an investor actually buying a property because they're so focused on getting all the cash out. I don't believe that 'recycling' the money system is the be-all and end-all. If you buy a high-yielding property, you're bringing money in. Use that to reinvest. That's what tops up your pot. Don't get googly eyed for what could happen over the next 6, 12 or 18 months. Yes, increase the value of your property, but also remember the market can turn quickly.

The market has decreased so quickly between mid-2022 to mid-2023. Good rental income is what is keeping money in your pocket and allowing you to invest again and again.

Higher ROCE will also entail a far more risky property, with so many more moving parts. Those projects also take a lot longer to find on the market. If a 0-15% ROCE can take 3-6 months to find, imagine how long it would take to find a higher ROCE?

Assess your risk levels and what risk you actually want to take on and also assess how quickly you want to find a property. Figure 1 gives a good indication of the different types of property deals associated with differing levels of ROCE. After all, the quicker you find a property, the quicker money starts arriving in your bank account.

Changing risk based on increasing ROCE

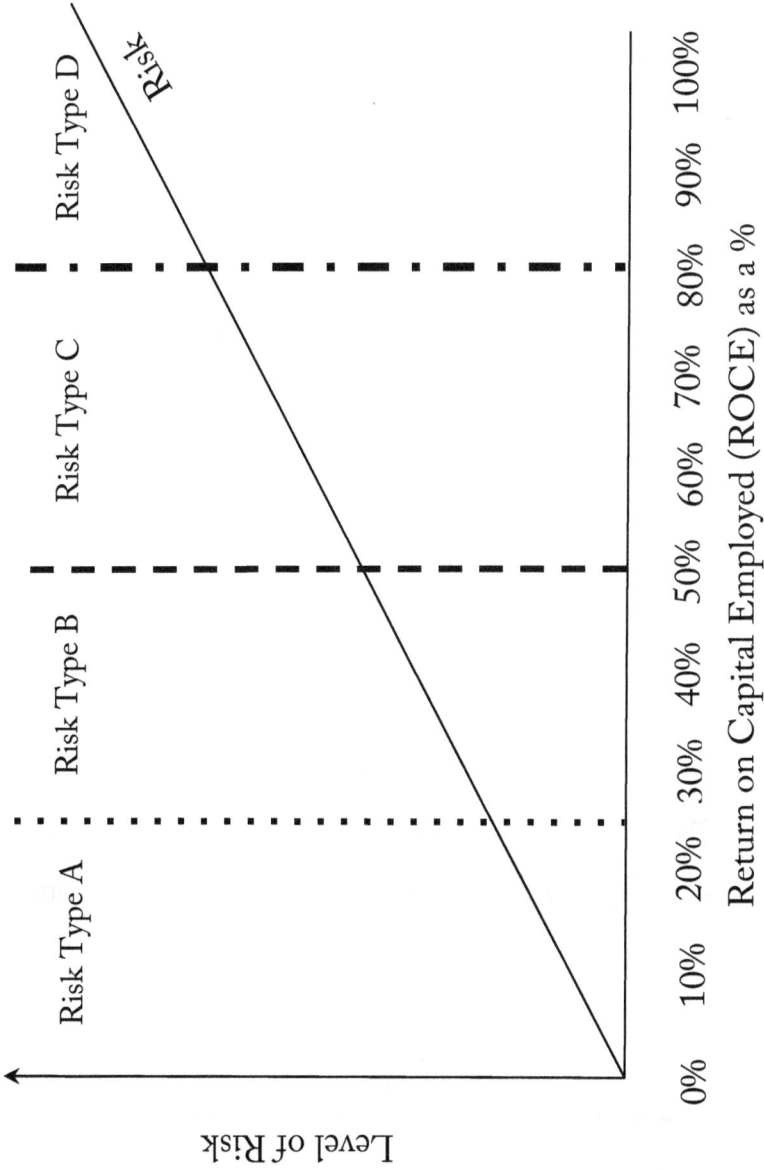

Risk Type A   Risk Type B   Risk Type C   Risk Type D

Risk

Level of Risk

0%   10%   20%   30%   40%   50%   60%   70%   80%   90%   100%

Return on Capital Employed (ROCE) as a %

Risk Type A: This would be a 75% - 100% tenanted building, with good tenants who can afford the rent and aren't going to cause you any management headaches. This is the type of building you can buy and hold and rely on a consistent income.

Risk Type B: This would be a 50% - 75% tenanted building, with average tenants. You need to expect to let several vacant units or do lease renewals or rent reviews in order to get a consistent income producing property.

Risk Type C: This would be a 0% - 50% tenanted building, with struggling tenants. You need to expect to let several or all of the vacant units or do lease renewals or rent reviews and sort out management problems in order to get a consistent income producing property.

Risk Type D: This building type will need a complete redevelopment in order to get a consistent income producing property.

A quick note here: Too often investors get caught on what other people are showing on social media or at networking events and want to do the same without ever thinking about what's going on behind the scenes.

The majority of investors I know who have big portfolios do not live off of their property income, me included.

Why? They want to keep growing their pot and they know that whilst they have different income streams, they are more secure, even if they shout about how much money they're making.

It doesn't make you a bad investor if you don't get all of your money out of a deal and you're not living financial freedom from your property empire after 12 months.

Trust me, the best investors are the ones that invest for the long-term and aren't embarrassed to get their income from elsewhere. It means they can take less risk and grow a portfolio of stable assets that will stand the test of time and economic swings.

That finishes up the chapter on goal setting. I hope you have some tangible goals to move forward into the rest of the book.

The Takeaway

1. Visualise your ideal future property investments with clarity.

2. Recognise your risk appetite and acknowledge that typically property investment is a long-term opportunity.

3. The detailed financial analysis of your situation–available cash, desired Loan to Value (LTV) ratio and target gross yield–will help you to establish clear and detailed investment goals.

4. Avoid setting arbitrary property numbers in your analysis.

5. Recognize the pivotal role of stable rental income in maintaining financial stability and prioritise consistent income streams.

6. Use the step-by-step guide to set your goals that can inform your decision-making and subsequent investment strategy.

7. Avoid comparing your progress with other investors. Everyone's situation is unique.

5

Market Analysis and Research

Before I get started, I want to make it clear that this isn't me giving you permission to dive into analysis paralysis. Far too many times I've seen clients get to this stage and flounder. They end up looking at all of the excuses for not getting into the commercial property market.

Nothing I will say in this book is going to get you to invest in commercial property if you don't actually want to invest in commercial property, or you are actively looking for an out.

All of the weaknesses and threats in the previous chapter will give you that out and you can do tons of research around those threats and weaknesses which could make you less likely to invest.

Think of it like the Facebook or Instagram algorithms. You research a topic, you see the posts, you linger on the post, the algorithm picks up that you may like the post and so starts delivering more of that content. You start liking the content, you get more of it. You save it, even more pops up, you comment and that's it. Those types of posts are all you see and then you never get another viewpoint.

You want different viewpoints. You want the good and the bad, the stuff you agree with and the stuff you don't. That's how you expand your horizons and why I already covered it.

Everything has a good and a bad—everything. When you invest, everything has risk, high and low. That's investing.

OK, lecture over from me. It is time to do some market analysis and research. Set yourself a time limit here and then decide to invest based on your knowledge.

Before we begin with the location specific part of the research, keep an eye on Base Rate changes, inflation and the general outlook on the economy. As I've said previously, this has a knock-on impact to yield and therefore a knock-on impact to price. You can take this a step further and read releases from the Bank of England and also subscribe to CoStar Alerts from costar.com, which will give you the headlines in the commercial property industry. I also recommend keeping track of politics insofar as reading manifestos and understanding how legislation may change if there is a party change, as this could be an opportunity or a threat. I also keep up-to-date with legislation and policy changes in regards to commercial property, as CoStar will usually have the headlines and then I'll read deeper. Property Week and the Estates Gazette are good subscriptions for this information, too. I personally also choose to read The Economist, but if I haven't got time one week, then it is not the end of the world. You can also listen to my podcast the Honest Property Investment Podcast for the best commercial property updates each week. And that is it, that's the end of my research. If you can spend 1-2 hours a week catching up on this information, you'll be in a prime position for understanding your location within the market.

And *then*, you should start by picking your investment location.

I firmly believe that picking the right location should be simple.

For me, it's a location either me or my family members go to regularly. Somewhere that has good transport links. A railway station is essential, as are bus routes and easy parking. I also want to see at least two large supermarkets within 1-2 miles of my search location, as this means that there are enough people in the area who need shopping, so there is some buzz going on. I also like to see major retailers in the area such as Boots, Domino's, McDonalds, Greggs, Starbucks or Costa. Again, it shows that there is local demand for these types of retailers. Ideally house prices would be rising in the area which shows that there is demand and it is becoming more affluent. I also want to invest somewhere the local council is investing money into, such as with their High Street Funds, or somewhere there are other large developers building in the area.

Locations I avoid are anywhere that is remote, with limited transport routes, or major cities: Manchester, London and city centre Birmingham (within 3 miles of the Bull Ring). The reason for avoiding major cities is because this is where large institutional investors operate and I'm not going to compete with them. I also won't get the yields that I want.

As a result, I'm very comfortable investing in the South West of England and the M5 corridor between Bristol and Birmingham and will target one search location every time I embark on a new search location.

I would encourage you to keep the locations you're searching in simple too. Start by looking within a 30 mile radius of your home town. Then create a checklist of non-negotiables that location has to have in order for you to want to invest there.

Examples:

- Train station
- Bus routes
- Lots of parking

- Increase in property values
- Good access to amenities such as schools, hospitals, parks, recreation
- A thriving downtown
- Low crime rates
- Property values increasing
- New infrastructure developments such as train lines or road connections, hospitals, parks, renewable energy, flood defences, sports stadiums, schools, housing estates etc.
- Supermarkets
- Certain retailers or businesses you deem to make an area successful
- Low vacancy rates for commercial property i.e. more than 80% of the retail premises have tenants (You can decide here)

TASK: Your task is to choose your own non-negotiable checklist of no more than 10 non-negotiables that your investment location *must* have.

Using the 30 mile radius of your home town, identify locations that have your non-negotiables.

Once you've got your investment location(s) sorted you have my permission to have a Google. Don't be shocked I'm saying this. We need to be aware of what's going on in the news, if anything. So, search 'Commercial property news in [insert location].'

I did this for Bath at the time of writing. I now know there are 20 new businesses opening in the city centre including homeware and clothes retailers, gift shops, food and drink outlets. I also know that vacancy rates for retail units in the city are now at 3-4% (Bath and North East Somerset Council, 2023).

Sleuthing a little bit more I found that a proposed new tenant in Southgate is Zara… oh my freaking goodness, finally. All it took was for Topshop and Boux Avenue to disappear and here they come–so long as the plans for signage are approved. Clocks ticking Bathnes council, we're waiting for a 'Yes' here (Bath and North East Somerset Council, 2023).

StoreAway is opening a 27,000 sq. ft. building on the London Road (Business Live, 2022).

In 2022, a large warehouse called Newark Works reopened its doors. Newark Works is a transformed Grade-II listed warehouse, offering 40,000 sq. ft. of flexible working space in Bath. It caters to independent businesses, providing a hub for creative companies of various sizes, including single entrepreneurs and larger, well-established firms, fostering a vibrant community within the city (Newark Works, 2022). Currently it looks like there is 17,000 sq. ft. still available of their bigger office spaces. The smaller ones have been snapped up.

Fangirling over big retailers finally making their way to my hometown aside, what did I learn through a 5-minute Google? Retailers are making a comeback in Bath and these bigger brands that I'm getting excited about will excite other people too and create a lot more footfall. Moreover, other industries are getting their foot in the door with storage and flexible offices popping up. Although, I'd only be looking at smaller office spaces if I was to go down that route.

This is all you want here, high level stuff. See what's going on. It feels quite exciting doesn't it? The thought of new possibilities running through a city you care about. Makes you want to invest.

Again, I reiterate: that was a 5-minute Google. It is not meant to give you the specifics. Remember this is what businesses and investors are bragging about, this is the hyped-up stuff.

Now let's move onto some more specifics.

My next port of call is always the Knight Frank Prime Yield Guides (2023). This is released monthly, around the 6th of each month, and notifies you of prime yields across all the different sectors and how market sentiment is trending. It is a free guide and should be on your 'must read' list as a commercial property investor.

I'm checking this out in May 2023 and I'm loving seeing the green positives back for the first time since pre-pandemic, especially in retail and out-of-town retail (long-term office lettings aren't faring so well, however).

How should you be interpreting this document? First go through the last column, see what has a weak market sentiment versus what's stable and positive. This then gives you an idea of what sectors are performing well right now.

You can then use this document as a guide for how yields are changing and you can estimate whether a building is priced correctly. For example, if you know that a high street retail unit is generating rent of £20,000 per annum in Bath and then you look at the yield guide and you identify that in May 2023, high street retail in prime towns are showing yields of 6.75%, I would add 1% onto the yield for risk to get to 7.25%. My next calculation would be 20,000 / 6.75% = £258,000. If the property was priced 10% either side of this, I know it's priced about right. If it is much higher, I know I'm going to have to negotiate.

Next, move onto SWOT (strengths, weaknesses, opportunities and threats) analysis of each of the locations you have picked. My starting place for this research would be ChatGPT. Shocked? If you ask ChatGPT to provide you with a SWOT analysis on commercial property in your location of choice, it will give you a brief overview, and you can then go digging from there. Now, it does have its faults. I typed in that I would like a SWOT analysis for Stroud, UK, which is a small location in the Cotswolds, and it stalled on me. But in this situation I asked for the pros and cons of Stroud and got some great answers. Also, ChatGPT doesn't have real time data so it can't tell you about market prices, yields or trends, however as a starting place it is fantastic.

This research will allow you to decide whether there is enough going on for you to want to invest there. Ultimately there is no right or wrong. I go back to the 5-year cycles of all commercial property, so you will have your ups and downs. You need to make your own choice about where it works for you.

That's all the details I need about an area. Now it's onto the data sites.

I know these websites are expensive, which is why I subscribe to them. And then, if our clients request the information, my team and I can send data to our Members Club clients.

First up is EIG Property Auctions. This is the most useful place to find what yields properties in your location transacted for. You can search past auctions and see what properties have sold for. To the right of the sold price, for properties which were let when purchased, you'll be able to see the rental income. Divide the rental income by the sold price to get the yield. With this yield, compare it to the yields that you saw from the Knight Frank Prime Yield Guide and see if the yields are similar. Building this picture will give you a range of yields that properties are selling for in the area. When you start to search for property investments, use the yield that is most comparably appropriate for your property type to gauge the value.

CoStar is also a very useful tool for getting sale price data and also leasing data for when you are researching how many properties have let recently. Similarly, Edozo or Nimbus Maps, which are aimed at individual landlords and priced accordingly, can also offer this type of information.

Again, I stress, signing-up for all of these pieces of software is expensive. Get a demo of all of them and pick the one which is most useful to you. Alternatively, as I said before, you're able to access all of this data in my Members Club.

Not All Locations Are Created Equal

Before we move onto the next chapter - the Property Search - I want to make sure you understand that not all locations are created equal in commercial property. You probably realised this if you went and looked at the Prime Yield Guides.

First, you have Prime areas. These are the most desirable locations in towns and cities. Usually, they are close to transport hubs as well as all major amenities. These are the most desirable locations, the place where the economy is the strongest, as people are moving in there whether to live or for business. They are also less risky places to invest, so you will find that the yields here are lower.

Secondary locations refer to areas that are considered less desirable or prestigious compared to prime locations.

These areas often have lower property values and may have fewer amenities or less developed infrastructure.

Secondary locations can vary depending on the specific market and city but they typically include areas that are farther from city centres, business districts or major transportation hubs. They may have lower foot traffic, less visibility or a less affluent demographic.

While secondary locations may not have the same level of demand as prime areas, they can still offer advantages for certain businesses. These locations may have lower rental or purchase prices, which can be attractive for cost-conscious businesses or those starting out. Additionally, some industries or businesses that do not rely heavily on foot traffic or depend on specific customer demographics may find secondary locations suitable for their operations.

It's worth noting that the classification of an area as primary or secondary can be subjective and may change over time. As cities grow and evolve, previously secondary locations may undergo redevelopment and revitalization, becoming more desirable and transitioning into prime areas. Secondary locations will have higher yields than prime locations.

Finally, tertiary locations refer to areas that are considered even less desirable or prestigious compared to both prime and secondary locations. These locations typically have lower property values, fewer amenities and less developed infrastructure compared to primary and secondary areas.

Tertiary locations are often found in the outskirts of cities or in less populated areas. They may be farther away from major transportation routes, business districts, or commercial centres. These areas may have limited access to public transportation and may lack the same level of visibility or foot traffic as prime or secondary locations.

Businesses that choose tertiary locations are typically motivated by lower costs, such as lower rental or purchase prices for commercial spaces. These locations may be suitable for businesses that do not heavily rely on customer walk-ins, such as warehouses, distribution centres or manufacturing facilities.

It is important to note that the classification of an area as tertiary can vary depending on the specific market and city. Additionally, as urban development expands, what was once considered a tertiary location may undergo changes and become more desirable or transition into a secondary location. Tertiary locations will have higher yields than secondary locations.

Towns and cities can also be classified as prime, secondary and tertiary. Within those towns and cities there will be prime, secondary and tertiary locations. Which means that you can choose your level of affordability and the risk you want to take. Remember the higher the yield, the riskier the property, however the more money that you'll be bringing in.

The Takeaway

1. Your investment decisions will be informed by both the macro- and micro-economic conditions. Macro conditions include inflation rate, Base Rate and the broader economic outlook. Micro conditions

include localised rental patterns, yield profiles and tenant churn.

2. Establish up to 10 non-negotiable characteristics for any location. This can help refine your search.

3. Think about potential locations known to you that are within a 30-mile radius. You may be able to visit them more readily.

4. Recognise that there is a hierarchy of locations in any town or city.

5. Desk-based research will help you establish the key facts that can inform your SWOT analysis.

6

The Property Search

You've now completed your market research on your chosen location, and it is time to get searching.

I'm not one of these guru types who gives you a really out-there strategy for finding commercial property.

One, because this will waste unnecessary time and two, because it is not necessary.

A question I get asked all the time is, 'Do commercial agents have little black books of buyers that they go out to first?'

The answer is yes.

How do you get on that list? You start searching for commercial property.

Yes, OK that sounds a bit chicken and egg, but hear me out with this simple strategy.

You should have your goal commercial property, which includes your target purchase price and the yield you are aiming for.

You've also just completed your market research, so you should have an idea what type of properties are achieving your desired yield.

Now, you need to set up search alerts on Right Move Commercial, LoopNet, Acuitus and EIG Auctions for your target property in your chosen location.

The simplest way of setting up search alerts is on Right Move Commercial. Set your search location to within 30 miles of your home and expand your search criteria to an asking price of 10% higher than your target price and 1% lower than your ideal yield.

Then, every time a property is sent through to you, go and see it.

I'm not joking, go see it. 'Boots on the ground', as Steve Wallis on our team likes to say. It is the most important way of showing that you actually want to invest in commercial property.

Go and talk to the agents in person. Show them you're interested. It is not only a great networking opportunity and also a fabulous learning opportunity. Mainly because you start to come to conclusions about what you like and dislike in various properties. It doesn't have to be rational. I know I could put certain properties in front of some clients and they would love them, but if the building looks slightly too concrete-y then it is a 'no', even if it makes the right yields.

You get to make that decision. Ultimately, if you get excited about a building you are more likely to actually work on it and move the mountains required to purchase it than if you are doing it purely for numbers and return. If you were doing this purely for that, you could probably find something else to invest in without leaving the comfort of your own home!

Now, what is important here is that you keep records on the properties that are being sent through to you from the search platforms. A property may not be the best opportunity now, but if it stays on the market for a few months, chances are it will have a price reduction or the seller may be willing to negotiate, in which case it may be the perfect property for you.

Here's how my team and I do it. We use Trello boards. On the Trello board, we have lists (similar to columns). The first list is 'Properties Looking at Currently', underneath this is a new card for each property we are looking at, which includes their address and a picture of the property. Information on the property is added to that card as we find out more about it.

The next list is 'Deal Analysis' then 'Inspection', 'Finance', 'Offer', 'Purchased', 'Come Back to in 3-6 Months Time' and finally, 'Doesn't Work for This Strategy or Sold to Other Parties.'

Properties that we're analysing are moved along the lists accordingly. Properties are never deleted as they are good evidence of what's going on in the market. Notes are kept on the exchanges with agents and thoughts on the deal itself, as well as how long it has been on the market and if it does sell to someone else, what it sells for.

This way, if it does come back to market, we can pounce on it. Alternatively, it is a great comparable and if you meet the agent doing the deal at another viewing it becomes a great conversation starter.

Tracking everything is the best move you can make here. Practice makes perfect, so it may be slow at first, but as you get used to putting this information together it gets quicker and quicker, so it can take as little as 15 minutes a day analysing deals. When you do make contact with agents to organise viewings, please make sure you get on their list of people to send deals to the minute they get something that's about to go on the market. That's the first step to going into that little black book.

The second step is - and I reiterate what I said before - talk to the agents at viewings. Tell them what you're looking for, how much money you've got in the bank and how ready you are to move on with the next deal. If you have time, take the agent to coffee, ask them about the local area and get some intel.

I'm a big fan of doing this. Yes, I love to chat as a first thing and I'm really interested in what other surveyors and property professionals are doing as I love the industry and find it exciting. I also get the low down on what yields properties are changing hands for and what has sold, as after all, the online databases are only as good as Land Registry and the websites data sleuthing team, so it can take a while for transactions to filter through. Information from those on the ground is gold dust.

You can add it to your market research and it gives you something to talk to the agent about, as you can ask them if they think it's true. You might find something out that you never expected, good and bad.

Plus, once you've had that conversation, the agent is more likely to give you a call when something comes to market and they'll ask if you want it. A quick sale is a win for the agent and their client. And, once an agent starts calling you when a deal comes to market, guess what? You're in their little black book.

I'm going to dial it back slightly. I've made this process sound very simple and it is. However, if you are just starting out, I understand it's not easy to pick up the phone and speak to a commercial agent or email them and ask for property details.

I suggest you do the following:

Email and say, 'Hi, I'm looking at property X. I would love to know if it is still available and what the viewing arrangements are as I'd like to have a look.'

Keep it short and simple and see if they come back to you within a few days. If not, pick up the phone and say, 'I'm following up on the email I sent on X date.'

That's your opening. Every investor, agent and surveyor does it. This is the best and most straightforward way to start the conversation.

I've put together a list of questions to ask, what to look for when you go for viewings and all the information you need so that you can do your due diligence properly. You can access this list and other free resources by scanning the QR code below. Add all of the information you've gathered from this list to your Trello board as you go.

The Takeaway

1. Having set your criteria, search efficiently.
2. Use various on-line platforms and arrange for alerts to be sent to you.

3. Take detailed notes and keep detailed records.

4. Build and maintain networks with local agents using various approaches.

7

Financing Commercial Property Investment

Financing commercial property investment is the part of commercial property that you will work on the hardest–that is if you need to finance it.

If you have cash available to buy commercial property, for example from your SSAS pension, it is always much easier to buy the property with cash and then restructure the deal into something that lenders want to lend on, because traditional mortgage lenders are picky!

If you are going to use traditional mortgage lending, you can expect to get a maximum Loan to Value of 70%. Although in the current economic climate that looks more like 65% as lenders are more risk-averse. As I said previously, interest rates are between 6.8-9%. If you are getting lending on your SSAS for less than £150,000, rates can be much higher—they can be up to 11%.

To give you an indication of SSAS lending terms, this was presented to one of my clients on the 27th April 2023:

- 1.5% arrangement fee
- 15-year term
- No Early repayment charges

With an interest rate of 4.6% above Base Rate or 3-year fixed at 9.04%

The requirements for this were:

- Last 2 years financial accounts
- Completed assets, income, liability and expenditure statement
- Sight of lease for the building – assuming 5 years remaining on the lease term, no breaks
- 6 months bank statements

- 3 months personal bank statements

Ouch, expensive! Plus the requirement for 5-year leases to be in place at purchase with no breaks. That's a lot to ask.

However, if you are looking for a larger loan then you can get slightly lower rates:

- 2% arrangement fee
- 3.49% above the Bank of England base rate.

The first of those loans was for £65,000 and the second for £500,000.

If the Base Rate goes up, the rates will go up inline with this. If you want up to a 50% loan to value then you can expect 1-1.5% lower rates.

That gives you a rough guide of where we are.

When you're shopping around for commercial mortgages, please make sure to ask multiple brokers to quote. Not all brokers are the same and it is wise to ask people you know who have already invested in commercial property for their recommendations. Don't just go for the broker who shouts loudly at networking events–there needs to be proof in the pudding.

It is important to realise not all lenders will lend on certain deals at certain times. Lenders have different risk appetites and also a set criteria for how much money they can place in certain types of property. If they turn your deal down, it doesn't mean it is a bad deal; if you can get your deal analysis to stack up, it just means they aren't the right fit for lending on that property. So, it is time to try someone else.

It is always a good idea to approach your own bank directly as well. High Street banks have commercial lending arms. For example, my bank is NatWest, they will always listen to a pitch about what I'm buying, however only once have I ever fit their criteria and that ended up being a residential property and not a commercial property. That's OK though, I'll still give my account manager a call and see what they can offer at the time, because when they do lend, it is at cheaper rates than you would get elsewhere because of the relationship they already had with you.

You also need to consider speed when you're going for lending.

Using investor finance is always the quickest route of funding. I have just completed a deal using investor finance and from start to finish the lending took one month.

Bridging can take a similar amount of time. Be warned though, some bridging lenders are doing very detailed due diligence and this can take months before they lend. Therefore speak to the lender to understand the time scales on lending.

Traditional bank lending can take 3-6 months to agree as there is a lot of due diligence that banks need to go through in order to lend to you.

Explain your needs to your broker and let them pick out a product that suits you.

For bridging fees expect a 2% arrangement fee and roughly 0.8% interest per month. There will be other fees on top of this which will be individual to each lender, so make sure to ask what those are.

Now, I've started with the bread and butter finance. So we can turn to a little bit more interesting finance.

For example, when I purchased 88 High Street, Barnstaple, I wanted to do it with No Money Down (I hate that term, but how else can I say it?). That deal was a £165,000 purchase with £15,000 coming in on a 5-year lease. I didn't have any money in the bank at the time.

How did I fund it? I assessed the rest of my portfolio and looked at where I had equity that I could use. Another one of my flats had £100k equity in it, but the mortgage fixed term wasn't due to expire for another 6 months, therefore I spoke to my broker who suggested we use a revolving credit facility.

Note: The revolving credit facility I used was through Just Cash Flow, who have since gone into administration, there are other options available for this type of facility

A revolving credit facility meant that they would take a second charge against my property and give me a pot of cash which I could draw down on as I wished. I could take £10,000 at a time, £30,000 at a time or the whole lot which was £70,000. I was then to pay interest on a monthly business of 1.5% of the amount I was to borrow. It was ridiculously expensive, however it worked for my purpose. I used this money to transfer it into my new limited company set up for 88 High Street and borrowed the rest on a 15-year mortgage at 7.29% interest rate with Shawbrook Bank.

Once that transaction had completed, I started the remortgage process on the flat that I had secured the second charge against, took the capital out to repay Just Cash Flow quickly so that I could come out of the short-term facility.

Please note that this only works where the mortgage lender who has the first charge allows a second charge to be put on the property as well. The lender that allowed it was NatWest.

Here's the costs for this transaction:

Purchase Costs		
	Property Purchase Price	£165,000.00
	Deposit	£65,530.00
	Stamp Duty Land Tax	£800.00
	Local Authority Search	£113.00
	Site Access Search	£219.00
	Drainage Water Search	£60.00
	Plan View Search	£90.00
	Land Registry Fees	£36.00
	Solicitors Fees (Second Charge)	£1,200.00
	Solicitors Fees (Purchase and finance)	£3,600.00
	NatWest Consent Fee	£100.00
	Land Registry fees (Second Charge)	£7.20
	Bank Transfer Fees	£18.00
	Indemnity Insurance (Enlargement of Title)	£100.00
	Indemnity Insurance (Listed)	£165.00
Shawbrook Fees	Lenders Arrangement Fee	£1,470.00
	Lenders Legal Fees	£1,140.00
	Lenders only indemnity policy	£174.34
	Lenders bank transfer fee	£20.00
	Companies House registration fee	£15.00
	Land Registry Registration fee	£95.00
	Funds transfer fee	£35.00

	Further Admin Fees	£8.40
	Structural Engineer	£1,275.00
Revolving Credit Facility	Mortgage Arrangement Fees	£0.00
	Arrangement Fee	£1,800.00
	Set Up legal costs	£0.00
	Total Purchase Costs	**£ 78,070.94**
Gross	**Return on Investment**	19.21%
Net	**Return on Investment**	9.56%

It was an interesting experiment in not putting any cash in the bank into a deal. However, it is a very expensive way of borrowing.

My best advice to you when it comes to lending is to go to a mortgage broker, explain the property deal and then what you want to get out of it, and give them all the details you've got on your current assets. From here, they'll be able to successfully match you to a product that will allow you to do the things you want to do.

My final piece of advice here is that I believe you can always find finance if the deal is right. Previously, I told you about my clever finance in Barnstaple. Now, let me tell you about my two commercial units in Bath.

It's a saga, so buckle in. I purchased the middle flat (out of three) in the building in 2015. There were two other long leaseholders in the building and I was happy to get on with them both (save for a mild disagreement about the pair of them breaking into my flat and cutting off the water supply, when it wasn't even my flat leaking).

The lady who had once owned the top floor flat had sadly died and her son was now in charge. He wasn't the landlord type and so was desperate to get some money out. In February 2020, he sold me the flat for £260,000... even though the value should have been £300,000+.

At the time, I agreed to an 80% loan-to-value mortgage. This required me to come up with a £52,000 deposit, which luckily came from the increase in value of another flat. The lender agreed to secure the mortgage against both flats, so I only needed to cover legal fees and Stamp Duty Land Tax.

I was pretty happy with this purchase. I let it to two nurses, and then Covid hit and lockdown happened.

That was the point in which the roof started to leak, badly. I mean, waterfall-through-the-building-type bad.

At the time, I didn't own the freehold. There was another party who owned the freehold and they had managing agents looking after the structure. I contacted them and contacted them, but they did nothing. In the end, I had my contractor get into the loft and patch as best as they could.

The freeholder, getting wind of my fix, told me I was under no circumstances to get on the roof and do anything.

2020 dragged into 2021 and nothing happened, my flats were getting damper and damper with every storm.

Eventually, in 2022 the nurses went to environmental health about the damp and environmental health stepped in. I explained the situation, but ultimately it fell on me to get it resolved. I ended up having to instruct my solicitors to take legal action against the freeholder for not doing the fix and causing excess damage, to which I wanted to be reimbursed all costs plus legal fees.

Side note, the council understood why I couldn't do anything apart from completely tarpaulin the inside of the loft so that no more water went through the flats. I dried the flats out with a dehumidifier and had them redecorated. At least the tenants were happy again.

This process was painfully slow and expensive, with each month seeing slow moving emails going backwards and forward between all involved.

I tried to negotiate to buy the freehold, which included the two commercial units, but the freeholder wasn't interested.

Until the start of 2023, when I received notice from the freeholder that they intended to sell the property at auction in July. To purchase it, I needed to declare my intention to buy and then match the highest bid at the auction.

The roof was still untouched and there was no sign of our legal dispute being settled.

Rather than keep throwing good money after bad, I waited for the property to come up at auction to see how much they wanted for it and what was in the legal pack.

Eventually, at the end of June 2023, the freehold and commercial units arrived at auction. By this time, I'd spent all of my savings on legal fees so I wasn't expecting to be able to buy the property.

I read through the legal pack anyway, noting that there was £24,500 per annum coming in. Based on my work in Bath I knew yields on property like this should be 7.5% and so I was expecting a guide price of £300,000 plus.

I was astonished when the guide price was only £200,000.

I read through the legal pack and noticed that the freeholder hadn't disclosed any information about my claim against them for the roof. I wondered, 'How would it be fair for this property to go to auction without all of the full facts?', So, I phoned the auction house and told them about the ongoing legal dispute and sent them evidence. The Auction House had to withdraw the freehold from auction because the information hadn't been disclosed.

Twenty-four hours later the auction house rang me and said 'How much do you want to buy the freehold for?' As a cheeky answer I said £200,000, the guide price.

I knew I was trying my luck but I thought that if I purchased at that much of a discounted rate, I'd be able to borrow 100% of the purchase price.

To my absolute surprise the freeholder agreed to sell it to me for £200,000 if I could exchange within 24 hours. Because of the spiralling legal claims I was, realistically, the only person he could sell it to.

No, I still didn't have the money. So I got to work. That afternoon I called every single broker and lender I could find. Going through the deal. Every time being asked, 'Why did they agree to sell it to you for £200,000 when it's worth £300,000?' and me answering, 'Because I'm suing them for a lot of money and no one else would buy it, so they just want it gone.'

I put 42 calls in that afternoon. Eventually one bridging lender replied to me and said they would sleep on it. Yes, I only had one potential lead out of 42.

At 9am, I still didn't have an answer. The freeholder was putting pressure on me to exchange and my solicitor was holding them off. By 10am, I had nothing.

I was still working to focus my mind on other things, but whenever anyone asked me how my day was going I told them I was on 'tenterhooks' over finding finance on this mind blowing deal which I couldn't let go.

Simply by sharing my story, one person said to me, 'If the bridging lender won't do it, I'll lend you £200,000 at 9% per annum until you remortgage'.

I'd found my finance, and also my solicitor found a mistake in the contract which meant that the contract had to be re-written, which meant we didn't end up completing the exchange until November.

I learnt here that telling others what you are doing can lead to opportunity. It also fully cemented my belief that if a deal is worth doing, finance will come along.

If you're wondering what happened to the roof, well I spent £2,000 on repairing slipped tiles and clearing the gutters and I don't have anymore leaks. Yes, all of that for a mere £2,000 worth of work.

For me it's been a fabulous deal, one commercial tenant has recently renewed a 5 year lease and the other still has 9 years left to run. Plus, I made £100,000 on Day 1, so I definitely can't complain!

Again, I reiterate: If you find a deal you can't let go of, you *will* find a way to work it out.

The Takeaway

1. Most purchases will require external funding.
2. Loan structures can be difficult to predict. It depends on the lenders' appetite for the deal.

3. Loans can take 3-6 months to complete – patience is needed.

4. Discuss your requirements with a number of brokers – their expertise and access to funds can vary considerably.

8

Deal Analysis

At this point you should have got to a place where you've started going out on viewings and collecting all of the information needed in order to do a deal analysis. Hint, this is all of the information I suggested that you collect in Appendix 1.

It's now time to work out if this deal is actually right for you.

Inside the Members Club, I have a course called 'Getting to Grips with Commercial Property Investment.' Within one of the training sessions is my full deal analysis spreadsheet. If, after reading this book, you are keen to continue with your commercial property journey, that is the place I would suggest you go next.

For now I'm going to give you access to a simple spreadsheet which you can access here by scanning the QR below.

In this spreadsheet you need to input the numbers in yellow. These include:

Potential Purchase Price	This is the amount you will be paying for the property
Current Rent Per Annum	The amount of rent that the property is currently generating. This needs to be rent only. If the rent is inclusive of other costs such as maintenance, utilities, business rates or any other costs outside of the rent then these amounts need to be deducted from the gross rent. Either you can estimate how much these costs are going to be on an annual basis or you can ask the seller

	for the accounts for the building from the last couple of years to see how much the landlord has spent on costs.
Estimated Market Rent	The amount of rent that the property could be generating if it was fully let. Again this is net of any costs that aren't rent that the landlord has to pay.
Loan to Value on Purchase (%)	Your target loan to value on finance when you purchase the property
Loan to Value at Market Value (%)	Your ideal loan to value if you were to refinance the property when the property is fully tenanted
Interest rate for long term lending (%)	The interest rate that you think you'd be able to get on a mortgage. Check with commercial property lenders like Shawbrook for this information
Are they FRI leases?	Full Repairing and Insuring Leases mean that the tenants are responsible for the maintenance of the building either themselves or through service charge. If you as the landlord will be paying for this as you are doing something like serviced office space then you will select no here.
Are you managing it yourself?	This is whether you are getting a managing agent involved or not.
Where are you purchasing the property?	England and Wales or Scotland as there are different Stamp Duty Land Tax regimes.

Will you be using bridging/short term finance to purchase the property so you can remortgage quickly to gain an uplift?	This is a yes or no question
How many months will you use bridging for?	If you aren't using bridging you can leave this
What interest rate per month will you be paying for bridging? (%)	Approach different lenders and ask what rates they are charging here
Will you be using a structural engineer?	This is a yes or no question
Will you be using a building surveyor?	This is a yes or no question
Refurbishment Costs	If you have a feel for how much this will be you can add a figure in here

This spreadsheet will crunch the numbers for you. Firstly, it will show you the net profit you are making on a monthly basis. It will show you the gross and net yields. It will also show you what your purchasing costs will be. If you are going to remortgage, then it will also allow you to forecast for any increase in capital value and rental value and what this will mean for your return on capital employed.

Based on your goals, you can make a decision as to whether this is right for you.

The spreadsheet also goes through a simple valuation calculation.

I must stress that this is not a Red Book Valuation. You can only do a Red Book Valuation if you are a qualified and a RICS Registered Valuer. However, what the calculation does is it allows you to calculate the rough value of the property at a very simple level.

Think back to what I said at the start: Rental income multiplied by the yield equals the capital value of the property. That's what we are doing here.

We are using the rental income and the appropriate yield to give us an estimated capital value.

To start off with, we need to know a few numbers:

1. Current rental income. How much income is the building currently producing?

2. Years that income is guaranteed for. In this case, you would work out how long there is left on the lease term; or if there is a break clause earlier, how long is left on the term until the break clause. After, calculate the average number of years left for all of the leases to run.

    - Note: My brain finds it easier to calculate this in months and then turn it into years. For example, if one lease has 18 months left and another has 26 months from today's date, I would add 18 and 26 together and divide by 2 (the number of leases in place) to get an average of 22 which is 1.83 years. If there isn't a lease in place or the property is empty then this figure will be 0.

3. The market yield, which you can get from comparable evidence or the Prime Yield Guides.

4. The future rental income if the property is fully let.

5. How long will it take to let the property on average?

6. How many months rent free you would need to give at the start of a lease?

   - Note: The answers for questions 5 and 6 you would get from local agents when you are doing your due diligence.

The Takeaway

1. The detailed analysis of recently completed sales provides important information that can be used in your own analysis.
2. Key information includes the yield, rental level and cost of funding.
3. Use the NCRE Spreadsheet linked in the chapter to do the number crunching.

9

Valuing Commercial Property

Now that you've done your calculations, we can get started with valuation. This method of valuation is called a Term and Reversion valuation, the reason being is that we are valuing the current income stream. This income stream is referred to as the Term, because that known rental income is coming in until a rent review or the lease ends. The Reversion is the potential future income stream after a rent review or new lease. Both the values are then adding them together to provide the property's Capital Value.

Please note that this is only the case for the commercial element of any property.

Initial Term Valuation: The valuation starts by assessing the present value of the expected cash flows associated with the initial term of the property using the Single Rate Years Purchase Multiplier.

The Single Rate Years' Purchase (SRYP) multiplier is a formula used to determine the present value of a future income stream. The SRYP multiplier formula is:

$$SRYP = [1 - \{1 / (1 + r)^{\wedge}n\}] / r$$

Where:

- SRYP is the Single Rate Years' Purchase multiplier
- r is the discount (yield) rate or interest rate
- n is the number of years over which the income stream will be received

In simpler terms, the formula calculates the present value of a future income stream by discounting the future cash flows by the discount rate. The discount rate represents the opportunity cost of investing money elsewhere or the current yield derived from recent market sales. The formula divides the present value of the income stream by the annual payment amount to determine the SRYP multiplier.

You will need the current rental income, years the income is guaranteed for and the market yield. In this example the current rental income will be £50,000, the years guaranteed for will be 2.5 years and the market yield will be 7%.

In the first part of the valuation, we will use the Single Rate Years' Purchase (SRYP) multiplier. The formula is initially shown with the yield and time inputs:

$[1- \{1 / (1 + 0.07)^{2.5}\}] / 0.07$

The important thing is to follow the correct sequence to establish the SRYP multiplier figure that is used in the valuation. There are four stages. You need to start with the (…) brackets, then the {…} brackets, thirdly the […] brackets and finally divide by the 7% yield.

STEP A: Calculating within the (...) brackets: (1 + 0.07)^2.5 = *1.184293769*

STEP B: Calculating within the {...} brackets: {1 / *1.184293769}* = *0.8443850896*

STEP C: Calculating within the [...] brackets: [1 - *0.8443850896]* = *0.1556149104*

STEP D: Divide the resolved [...] brackets by the yield: *0.1556149104* / 0.07 = *2.223070149*

The SRYP multiplier in Step D is rounded to 4 decimal places: 2.2231

The value of the current income stream (£50,000) is found by multiplying it by the calculated SRYP multiplier: 50,000 x 2.2231 = £111,153.51

The next step of this appraisal is to do the Reversion element of the valuation. This is now valuing the income stream after the current term comes to an end.

You will need the market rent for the property, years in which it will be received (hint: this is the same as the years the rent is guaranteed for in the term valuation) and the yield for the reversionary rent. In this example, the market rental income will be £650,000, the years until the rental income will be received will be 2.5 years and the yield for the reversionary rent will be 9%. Usually, the yield for the reversionary rent will be 1-2% higher than the market yield because the rental income in the future is more risky, it hasn't yet been agreed.

Here's the calculation you will use:

You start by working out the Years Purchase (YP) multiplier. This is very simply, 100 divided by the yield for the reversionary rent.

YP Multiplier: 100 / 9 = 11.1111

You then work out the value of the future income stream which is £60,000 x 11.1111 = £666,666.67.

You then discount this amount by anticipated costs of reletting fees. We assume this to be 2.6% which would cover legal and professional lease renewal fees.

£666,666.67 x 2.6% = £17,333.33

The figure net of reletting fees is £666,666.67 - £17,333.33 = £649,772.58

At this point, you can then deduct from the analysis any capital costs that you are looking to spend. For example, if you are looking to spend £60,000 on capital costs, these include costs for EPC improvement works, or maybe you need a new roof, etc. Whatever it may be, your sum would be:

£649,772.58 - £60,000 = £589,772.58

Your next step is to then calculate the discount in the number of years until you receive this income.

To calculate the number of years, you add the years until the rental income will be received plus the number of years it will take to let the property (for example 6 months = 0.5 years) and the amount of rent free you'd be offering (for example 3 months = 0.25 years).

Therefore, if you were going to receive the reversionary rent in 2.5 years after the current leases have come to an end, with a 3-month void period and a 3-month rent free you would be receiving this rent in 3-years time.

You then need to calculate the present value of the capital value of the rental income, so essentially (following this example) what the value of £589,772.58 would be in 3-years time.

The present value formula is a mathematical equation used to calculate the present value of a future cash flow. It takes into account the time value of money, which means that money available in the present is considered more valuable than the same amount of money in the future due to factors such as inflation and the opportunity cost of not having access to the funds immediately.

The general formula for calculating the present value (PV) is:

$$PV = FV / (1 + r)^n$$

Where:

- PV is the present value

- FV is the future value or the amount of money to be received or paid in the future

- r is the discount rate or the rate of return that reflects the time value of money and other factors

- n is the number of time periods or the length of time until the future cash flow is received or paid

By dividing the future value by the discount rate raised to the power of the number of time periods, the formula discounts the future cash flow to its equivalent present value.

First we need to start by getting the Present Value rate. To do this we would do the following calculation:

1 / ((1+(**3**)%)^**3**) = 0.9151416594

In that calculation the only number you change is the 3, which I've put in bold twice. This refers to the number of years until you receive this number. The 0.9151416594 is the present value (PV) rate.

You then multiply the present value rate 0.9151416594 x £589,772.58 = £539,725.46

£539,725.46 is the reversion value, the value of the income stream after the current rental income stream comes to an end.

Then you need to add the term value (the value of the current rental stream) and the reversion value together.

£111,153.51 + £539,725.46 = £650,878.96, which gives you an estimated valuation for the commercial property.

You can then round that figure to the nearest ten or five thousand pounds

In the example above it would be £650,000.

This is the maximum you should be offering or paying for the property. In fact, I would be discounting this in the amount that you are offering and starting 20%-30% lower to give yourself room to manoeuvre.

Also remember to add this figure back into your deal analysis and see if the deal analysis stacks up as a purchase price.

It may seem like I threw a lot at you just there and it can take a while to go through, so I suggest reading through this chapter a couple of times. Also, download the spreadsheet, as the calculations are on there for you to use.

A step on from this is Vacant Possession Value.

Mortgage lenders are asking valuers to value properties on Vacant Possession Value and then for some mortgage lenders, they are lending based upon vacant possession value.

Vacant Possession Value, for the most part, is less than Market Value, which is the valuation we've just done.

Why?

Well, it doesn't include the term part of the valuation. It assumes that at the time of purchase the property will be empty and therefore there is no current income stream to value.

Instead, the valuation is the reversion value as we've just completed above. Usually an extra 1-2% is added to the yield and the vacant occupancy time period is longer. This void period has to be based on current market evidence, so it is a good idea to phone local agents to find out what the anticipated vacant period may be and what sort of rent free periods they are offering tenants as an incentive to come into the building so that this can be discounted from the value.

When calculating Vacant Possession Value, you should again be including any capital costs required to make the building lettable.

Now, in some rare cases, Vacant Possession Value may be higher than current Market Value. This will only happen when market rents have gone up and therefore it would be a better option to get the current tenants out and re-let to new tenants at a higher rate. You'll see this in an increasing market.

The other point to note on valuations: Once a building is let and you've just agreed all of the leases and the rent, you can assume that you've agreed it at market rent. Therefore, at this point you assume you could get this rent forever, because if you were able to get rent that was any different, surely you would have agreed to it, right?!

At this point in a building's life-cycle you can do a simple valuation which is rental income divided by the yield to get the rough approximation of value. Why no discounting? Well, it is assumed you have already completed any capital expenditure prior to the lettings and there isn't going to be void periods because the leases have just been agreed. This is when the building should be at its highest possible value. Essentially, it is the point in time when you are likely to get the rent in for a long time. It is the least risky time of the leases, so the yield is lower and the rent should be at its maximum level.

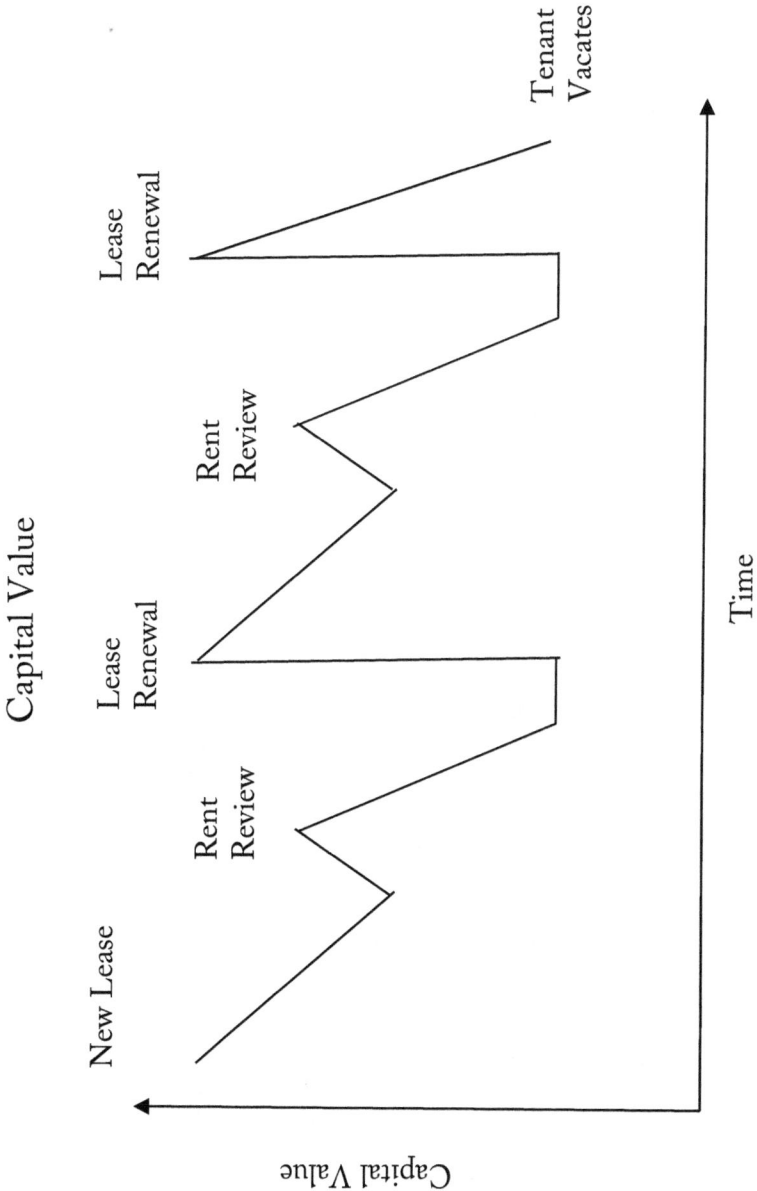

Capital Value

New Lease
Rent Review
Lease Renewal
Rent Review
Lease Renewal
Tenant Vacates

Capital Value

Time

I explain that in more detail in the Capital Value diagram. Now, just to be clear, this diagram shows excessive movement in values. Don't worry, your commercial property value isn't going to fluctuate excessively. However, every time you move your leases back to market rent and at the end of the lease, extend the amount of time left for that rental income to come in, (i.e. put in place a new 3-, 5- or even 10-year terms) you're increasing the value of the property.

The Takeaway

1. The valuation of commercial property uses discounting formulae that have rent, yield and time inputs.
2. It is vital to establish the Years Purchase multiplier that is used to capitalise the rental income.
3. Different opportunities will require different types of valuations, but all use discounting formulae.
4. Use the NCRE Deal Analysis spreadsheet to inform your decision-making.

5. Your valuations can act as a guide for property selection and negotiation.

6. If you are funding the purchase externally, the lender will require a valuation to be undertaken by a RICS Registered Valuer–at your expense.

10

Offering on a Property

You now understand how to complete a deal appraisal and value a property. Now it's working out how to make the property work for you and your goals and where you should be offering.

I have to stress here: To become a commercial property investor, you *must* offer on property.

I repeat: To become a commercial property investor, you MUST offer on property.

This stage is mandatory. Far too often would-be investors come to me and say they want to buy commercial property but they can't find the right one. I then ask, how many properties they've offered on. The answer? None.

Please don't let that be you.

The other mindset shift that you need to make here is that agents honestly don't care what price you offer at. Again, I get told so often that would-be investors feel embarrassed or feel that they won't get taken seriously if they offer too low. The agent doesn't care and also, it's none of your business if they do. In the investment space you need to look after yourself and your investment business.

Doing the deal analysis and then the valuation should allow you to identify what your ideal purchase price is to hit your goals. Your job is to then work backwards from that and offer lower so that inevitably, when the sellers agent comes back and counters or says no, you've got somewhere to go.

When I'm putting in an offer for myself or for a client I always start with a phone call to the agent. I talk to them and say that I like the building and I've been crunching the numbers and I'm going to be offering around £X. Then, I judge the feedback. If the agent umms and ahhs, I say, 'What would get the seller to accept my offer?' If they give you a steer towards what the seller would accept, either I think, 'Great, that falls in line with what I'm about to offer' or I consider whether I would change my offer to get it closer to the client's expectations.

I finish the phone call explaining what I'm going to do next. For example, I say, 'I'm going to send in an offer letter by X time today.'

I then do what I say I'm going to do. That's important. Do what you say you're going to do. That's when you're taken seriously.

I've added a template offer letter in my free downloads which you can access by scanning the QR code:

That offer letter will show you are serious and that you've thought through every eventuality. Your offer may not be accepted the first time, but the agent will respond to this and that gets you in the game.

Once your offer is accepted, you will receive the heads of terms from the sellers agents and this will also be circulated to both sides of solicitors. The solicitors will start the legal process.

Your job is to do further due diligence.

Just remember that the amount that you agree to pay in the offer often won't be the amount you pay on completion. The reason being that your due diligence will probably lead to you asking for deductions or changes to the contract. It's expected.

For example, when my client purchased a property in Cornwall, the original figure was £580,000. After the building survey, we discovered there were problems with one of the roof lanterns, so we agreed to shave £5,000 off of the purchase price.

Alternatively, if you discover the seller hasn't got the reports you require such as a fire risk assessment, you can request they do this during the conveyancing period and either ask them to put the necessary fire safety in place or get a deduction from the price for you to be able to do this. It's law, they should have already done it, so the fact they haven't requires that discount.

Similarly, with Energy Performance Certificates, if you've requested the seller get an EPC completed and it comes back with an F or G rating you could ask for the seller to do the work to get it up to an E rating or you could get a deduction to do it yourself.

This is why a building survey is a great tool to have, as this will tell you where any defects or problems are and will give you a rough cost to fix it. Once you have this, you can then take it a step further and get contractors in to quote for the work, or get architects to put together plans for your new scheme.

You may not always have time to get a building survey, for example during an auction purchase, but when you go to an auction, factor in any potential costs so that you can deduct this from your maximum offer.

It may also be that you're buying a commercial property where all the leases are full repairing and insuring leases. In this case a building survey may not be needed because the tenants will be paying for any maintenance on the building.

You also need to make sure that you insure your property from exchange, so it's wise during the due diligence process to check that you can get insurance. Should anything come up which insurers aren't happy with, you can get the seller to resolve it. Note here: If it turns out the building is uninsurable for any reason that you won't be able to solve, pull out.

Finally, if you are requiring lending, the lender is going to have a number of requests which will form part of their due diligence. You will need to find out this information from the seller in order to get lending. If the documentation the lender requires isn't available, chances are they aren't going to lend or they will withhold some of the amount they're lending until they're satisfied that they've got all of the necessary documents. Your solicitor will also be doing due diligence too and will be letting you know what they are happy with and what they are not happy with. They too want to make sure you're buying a watertight investment, so make sure you listen to advice here.

Ultimately the period between an offer being accepted and actually completing a deal is a long one. Use this time to find out every single little detail about the building. Where you're not happy, get the seller to either sort it out, or negotiate a discount. Only complete when you're 100% satisfied you're buying the investment you thought you were.

Something that usually comes up around this time of the investment process is market research and demand for space. If you buy a fully let building this won't be so much of a problem. However, if you are looking at a building with vacant space, this research is necessary.

You can take a number of routes for figuring out demand. Look at vacancy rates in the area, not just empty shops. Think back to earlier in the book when I was researching Bath and discovered Zara is taking the old Topshop and Boux Avenue units. Well, those units have been empty for ages, so just by looking at the retail parade I would have thought that the South Gate area is becoming a ghost town and there's no take up. Whereas behind the scenes there is a letting bubbling. Phone agents and find out what's really going on. Ask them what take-up for the type of space you're going to be offering will be like.

Next up, you can go and get into the market. Go to the local Chamber of Commerce meetings or local entrepreneur meetings. Find these business groups on LinkedIn in or Facebook and ask if anyone would be interested in the space that you are going to be bringing to the market shortly.

Create a Facebook Page for the building and explain that in 6, 12, 18 months time this is coming to the rental market. Put mockup photos, explain the size and then create a waitlist. Ask potentially interested tenants what space they are looking for and how much would they pay for it. You could even put some advertising credit behind it to get out to a wider audience.

You aren't going to be 100% sure that you will get immediate take up on space you bring to the market, but by doing this research you can get to 80%! Your job is to then create spaces that these businesses want to be in.

The Takeaway

1. Commercial property investors MUST make offers on properties.
2. Use the Offer Letter Template or amend it to suit.
3. You owe it to yourself to undertake due diligence checks – EPC status, Fire Risk Assessment, full rebuilding insurance cover, correct use under planning – before committing to a property.
4. Use social media platforms for current market trends and space demand profiles.
5. The time between acceptance of an offer and completion of the transaction can be lengthy – ensure that full rebuilding insurance and site security are in place.

11

Property Management

Woohoo, at this point I'm assuming you've purchased the property. Now the fun stuff starts.

I believe wholeheartedly that property management is the backbone of building a successful commercial property portfolio. If you can be a great property manager, or hire a great property manager (ahem, someone like my team at Team NCRE) then you are going to have a property portfolio that continuously grows.

Property management in commercial property is all about the landlord - tenant relationship. You handle this well, you're onto a winner. The lease dictates that relationship. The lease will set out who's responsible for what, the landlord or the tenant. Whether that's repair, maintenance and decoration, rebuilding insurance or any number of other things.

At this point, I'm going to pause and tell you what you shouldn't do in this situation because it can ruin everything. Don't be nice. It can be really easy to buy a building and have loads of tenants in there. You go in with grand ideas of putting service charges in place and renegotiating on the leases to get longer terms and market rent. You're determined, but the tenants get to you. They start emailing and texting about how bad the previous landlord was and that there is X, Y and Z problems (usually a leak) and all of a sudden you're sucked into their gloom and you feel awful that you bought a property with problems. You know your next step is going to be to renegotiate leases with them so that they don't think that you're the bad landlord too. Then, you start picking up costs or telling them that everything is going to be OK and you pander to their 'pain'. By the end of it, you're exhausted, feel like you have a dud deal and all of your funds have been depleted.

I've seen this happen on too many occasions to count. One particularly bad property was in Cornwall. We'd purchased this property for a client in 2021 because all of the leases were full repairing and insuring, and most leases were 5 years plus. However, the seller had only ever billed a few hundred pounds in service charge here and there over the years.

When my client purchased it, we hit the ground running. We got a building survey with the details of what needed to go through the service charge over the next 5 years. We then split the costs into a 5 year maintenance plan, which worked out at roughly billing the tenants a combined £20,000 per annum or £3.66 per square foot, starting in 2022.

The push back we got was wild. The tenants were up in arms about this, even though their leases stated they had to pay. The tenants wouldn't talk to us, 'the surveyors', about this, instead they went straight to the landlord, who, feeling sorry for them, picked up a huge amount of the cost of bills to try and placate the tenants for *years* (yes, even in the 2023/2024 service charge year). It didn't work, they still hated paying service charges and knowing that the landlord would open their purse, the tenants pushed it and pushed it. The difference in income from the fallout of this was that the building was meant to be generating a 10% yield, but in the end, with all the expenses and the tenants not playing ball, it looked more like a 5% yield. Definitely not worth it!

This comes from being too nice and wanting to be seen as good. But who are you being good to? Yourself or the tenants? Usually the tenants, but why? Because you want to please people.

That does not and should not happen in commercial property management. Yes, speak to the tenants. Yes, they are always going to tell you the worst things that are happening in the building

But remember, they're still in the building. They're still trading. So that is a good sign that they want to make things work, so roll with that.

Before you buy a commercial property you should know what it says in each of the leases. So, you have your eyes wide open to your responsibilities when you come into the building and what you need to tell the tenants to do themselves. Essentially, what do the leases say about service charges?

The lesson is: If there is a service charge provision in the lease, charge service charge.

I'm going to repeat this so those at the back can hear. **If there is a service charge provision in the lease, invoke the service charge.**

Why? So that the tenants can budget for this. If the lease has a service charge clause but the tenant gets used to not paying it, guess what? They are going to be deeply unhappy and not pay the service charge when you try charging it in future.

So do it properly from the start. As surveyors, we have to follow service charges in Commercial Property (RICS, 2023), as this is the professional guidance explaining exactly how we operate.

We must put in place a service charge budget at least one month before the service charge year starts and send it around to the tenants so that they know what it is that they will be paying in the upcoming year.

The lease will often specify the date of the service charge year. However, if it doesn't, you can decide the start date of the service charge year. Ideally, you'd at least start it on the 1st of a month.

Then you need to look at how the service charge will be apportioned. Some leases set out a service charge percentage of the occupational space or even a set amount that a tenant should contribute towards the service charge.

If the lease is silent on this, you can apportion the service charge. This is usually done on floor areas and is a percentage of the total floor area that the tenant takes up within a building. You can get a surveyor to come out and measure the building for you if you don't have these areas and then you can show this to your tenants so there is no dispute.

Next up, you need to think about how much to charge and what you are going to charge for. You must follow the lease as a guide here. The lease will specify what can be charged through the service charge. In an ideal world, all tenants in the same building would have uniform service charge clauses in their leases, in which case it's all the same. However, please read each of the leases to make sure they are the same. If they are different then this will need to be reflected in what you charge the tenant.

Service charges in Commercial Property are really useful for identifying what you can charge for. In the appendix, there is a breakdown of all the different costs. Use this as a starting point.

You then need to go and get quotes for the different services that you are going to need to implement. Fire safety, electrical safety, gas safety, routine gutter and drainage clearance, cleaning of the common parts and windows, where there are common toilets or kitchen, restocking these, etc. Electricity, gas and water charges for the common parts need to be recovered through the service charge. You need to budget for maintenance of any lifts or escalators and door entry and security systems. You need to make sure you have appropriate commercial waste disposal in place and agree that cost with the local council. Pest control is also something to consider, as well as outside lighting to make sure that both tenants and their customers can see where they are going and there is less of a risk of someone falling or injuring themselves and you having to deal with this through the insurance. Gardening and landscaping services can also be useful if you have any garden area or plants, to keep that looking nice. If you have a carpark, entry control systems and security should have an appropriately sized budget. Finally, you need to budget for maintenance, both planned and reactive maintenance.

Planned maintenance is maintenance that you schedule in across a 5-10 year period. To work out what maintenance is needed and how much this should cost, you should instruct a building surveyor to go and assess the building and identify maintenance needs and costs and when the maintenance needs to be completed. You can then forecast how much you need to add in the budget for planned maintenance over the next couple of years. You can also put the cost of the building surveyor through the service charge as well.

Reactive maintenance or emergency repairs are things that you can't plan for. This is where the tenant calls you up and tells you that something has gone wrong in the building. I would suggest budgeting 10-20% of the total service charge budget for this.

Once you've completed the budget, you can then bill the tenants at the intervals it specifies in the lease. Either all upfront, monthly, quarterly or half-yearly.

At the end of the service charge year you need to complete the service charge accounts. This identifies actual expenditure. If the amount you spent on through the service charge is less than you collected you refund the tenants the amount they've overpaid. If you didn't charge the tenants enough then you need to bill them for the difference. This must be done within 4 months of the service charge year coming to an end.

If you don't have a service charge provision in the lease and the lease states that the tenant isn't responsible for the structure and common parts of the building but only their own occupational space, you will be responsible for those costs as the landlord.

I would still suggest you budget for these costs. Far too often landlords are reactive and just pick up maintenance costs as they go. The expenditure for a building surveyor to come and put together a building maintenance plan is still so necessary. This way you can forecast your income from rent and when you can afford to spend on maintenance that needs completing. Maintenance is also far less expensive when you do it before a catastrophe happens.

A well-maintained property also maintains the value of the property. If you think back to when we looked at valuations and we discounted the reversion value for capital expenditure needed to get the building into lettable condition. If you want to maintain value, keep your building in lettable condition so those hefty discounts don't need to be applied to the value.

As I alluded to earlier, the tenants will have their own demised area and usually, unless they are on licences, they are responsible for their demised area. This means any maintenance, running costs such as utilities and business rates and health and safety are things that tenants are responsible for and they often need to be reminded of this. Especially when it comes to fire safety, every tenant should get their own fire risk assessment for their unit. You as the landlord will get a fire risk assessment for the common parts, tenants must get a fire risk assessment for their unit. Both parties should work together to ensure that all of the recommendations for improving fire safety are completed within the time scale designated. The documentation must be kept on file for rebuilding insurance purposes and in case the local authority's environmental health officers or the fire and rescue service make unannounced visits (yes this does happen and if you have multiple properties they will want to see the fire safety compliance for all properties).

Talking of health and safety, what do you actually have to adhere to in Commercial Property? It's very similar to residential property in this regard. In the free resources for this book I've added an overview of all the health and safety protocols you need to adhere to, so you can download this and follow it. You can access these resources by scanning the QR code below:

You're probably thinking, 'Natasha, this is a lot!' Yup, that's why for many landlords, as their portfolio grows, they outsource this element because running and managing the day-to-day element of a commercial property portfolio takes a lot of time and commitment. Good communication with the tenants and finding some awesome contractors who are going to come out and service the building will help loads.

One big recommendation I have for you is, if you are going at it alone on property management, make sure you have key safes at the building with all the keys labelled. What you should also do is have a reporting method for contractors to inform you that they've collected and returned the keys. The contractors must also know what will happen if they don't return the keys (i.e. there is a penalty they must pick up). This simple organisational tool can save you so much time and effort. Plus, if you are then super-organised, you will have a secondary, back-up key safe in case any keys do go missing. I use a company called the Key Holding Company in the UK who also look after my keys and can go out and sort out any key issues or open doors if necessary.

As an overview to property management, your job as a Landlord is to know who is responsible for what aspect of the building, so that if a tenant calls you, you can bat back at them anything that is their responsibility. Where there are common areas, check the lease and see if there is a service charge. Where there is a service charge, make sure you budget and charge so that the building is well-maintained. Finally, make sure you're adhering to health and safety. This is absolutely mandatory as you could end up with huge fines, jail time or what's worse, killing someone. It is your responsibility as a landlord to look after this, so make sure that you do!

If you get property management right, you will significantly increase the value of your building. Firstly, because as a landlord you won't be paying for any expenses and this is valuable at sale. Secondly, that great landlord-tenant relationship makes it easier to maintain the building so its always in good condition plus, a well-maintained building with a great landlord will mean tenants want to stay and keep paying rent. Again, a win-win for all involved.

The Takeaway

1. Recognise that property management is crucial for building a successful commercial property portfolio.
2. A strong landlord-tenant relationship is at the core of effective property management but also for tenant satisfaction and investment performance.
3. Understand that the lease document is of critical importance in the relationship.
4. Implement the service charge to all who should be contributing.

5. Draft proactive maintenance schedules and make financial provision for reactive repairs.

6. Strictly comply with health and safety regulations - fire safety measures, Energy Performance Certificates (EPCs), gas safety checks, electrical safety checks, asbestos checks, water-borne risks such as Legionella.

7. As your portfolio grows, consider outsourcing your property management.

12

Commercial Property Leases

I had thought about starting this chapter with: 'Commercial property leases dictate the landlord/tenant relationship'. Essentially, how you manage a property will be set out in a lease. Therefore, you want to make sure that you have terms clearly set out in each lease so that both the landlord and the tenant understands what responsibility each has.

That statement is completely true. But I'm sure I was about to bore you to tears. Please don't tune out.

Leases create value in your property.

Going back to the valuation of a commercial property: the lower the risk of the property and thus the lower the risk of you not receiving rent, the lower the yield your commercial property is valued on, and so the higher its value.

So, the whole plan with a lease is to make sure that you are securing the rent for as long a period of time as possible *and* where possible, putting in place mechanisms to review the rent to the best of either the current market rent or a higher market rent, whether that's based on an open market valuation or a recognised published government index (Consumer Price Index or Retail Price Index) or an agreed percentage uplift.

Plus, you want to sprinkle some more security for yourself as the landlord in there by adding a rent deposit and a guarantor or personal guarantee from the tenant.

Then, take it a step further by making sure the tenant is responsible for maintenance, either via paying for the cost of works to the structure and common parts themselves if they are the only tenant or via a service charge if they are in a building with multiple tenants.

Therefore, we see the following lease clauses as landlord-friendly clauses, because these are leases clauses which can increase the value of the property:

- Longer leases, generally 5 years or more

- Rent reviews which either allow the rent to stay the same or increase

- Maintenance clauses which make the tenant responsible to pay for the maintenance of the structure of the building as well as their own unit

- Deposits and/or guarantors

While there are landlord-friendly clauses, it means that there are also tenant-friendly clauses. These range from leases where the tenant doesn't have to pay for any expenses on the building other than rent (i.e they have an all-inclusive rental figure). They have the option to break the lease at any point before the term is up. The rent review goes either up or down, or there is no rent review.

If the tenants want more tenant-friendly lease clauses then arguably they should pay a higher rent for these privileges as it could impact the value of the property. For example, if the tenant has a break after Year 1 then the term certain on that rent is only 1 year and that's higher risk than term certain of year 5.

As a rule of thumb, I add 5% of the annual rent to every tenant friendly-lease clause that is given to them when agreeing on the lease. They may not agree to it, but it is a good starting point for negotiation!

Please note that at this point I have to highlight that you must be fair when negotiating on leases. Luckily the RICS has you covered for this in its Code for Leasing Business Premises, 1st edition.

> "The objective [of this code] is to improve the quality and fairness of negotiations on lease terms and to promote the issue of comprehensive heads of terms that should make the legal drafting process more efficient. The statement and code do not prescribe the outcome, but seek to make it fair and balanced by identifying the terms that are usually important and encouraging

both parties to obtain advice from property professionals. This enables negotiations to proceed properly so that each party can make an informed decision about whether to proceed on the terms that they negotiate." (RICS, 2022)

This is the most user-friendly code the RICS has put together so I highly recommend you read it. Now that I've given you the terms that are more landlord-friendly, use it to understand how negotiations work and the other terms that you can throw in there. The other terms are relatively neutral in terms of the valuation of your property.

A feature of the current valuation market is that valuations are being discounted for low EPC ratings to accommodate for the cost of getting a property to minimum energy efficient standards

What I would suggest is that when agreeing to a new lease with a tenant, you always offer the best possible scenario for you and see what the tenant comes back with. From there you can look to negotiate.

NC Real Estate has recently had this experience when renewing 8 leases in the same building

Ideally the client wanted straight 5-year terms but we knew that not all tenants would be happy with this as we were looking to get them off of one-year rolling leases. Therefore we offered the tenants 3 options in terms of the leases that they could take:

Option 1: 5-year lease with break option after 3 years

Stepped rent: (insert specific levels here per unit)

Year 1:

Year 2:

Year 3:

Years 4&5

Break option at the end of year 3 subject to a 6 month notice, full payment of rent and service charge, and leaving the unit free of tenant's belongings, empty and free of any third party occupations

Rent free period: 1 month granted at the commencement of year 4

Option 2: 5-year lease with break option after 2 years

Stepped rent: (insert specific levels here per unit)

Year 1:

Year 2:

Years 3-5:

Break option at the end of year 2 subject to a 6 month notice, full payment of rent and service charge, and giving up occupation, leaving the unit free of tenant's belongings, empty and free of any third party occupations

Rent free period: ½ month granted at the commencement of year 3

Option 3: 5-year lease with no break option

A straight 5-year option is still available, at a reduced rent from the original proposal of £XXXX

The tenants could then pick what they wanted. Interestingly we had a mix of all three options signed, which meant on average, the rent as a whole was guaranteed for at least 3 years which was a result for my client's valuation.

OK, so we know about the lease terms you can offer, now let's go back to the theory behind leases because you do need to know it.

It is important to be aware at this point that there are different laws which govern leases in Scotland vs England and Wales.

English and Scottish leases contain similar provisions, such as repair, decoration, alienation, alterations, permitted use and forfeiture (irritancy).

England and Wales the Landlord and Tenant Act 1954 (the 1954 Act) gives commercial tenants security of tenure and there are strict procedures which must be complied with before renewing a lease. Whereas in Scotland, even when there is a contracted expiry date, if the parties do nothing to terminate the lease, it will be implied that the lease will continue for a further year after the end of the contractual term. This is known as 'tacit relocation'.

It is usual for a landlord to give the tenant at least 40 days written notice that it wishes the lease to end upon expiry of the contracted term.

Scotland is simple.

England and Wales…are not.

In England and Wales, business tenancies are governed by the Landlord and Tenant Act 1954 Part II.

Back in 2017, I wrote a really successful blog post about 1954 Act Leases, which has shown up in many an assignment that students used to hand me when I was lecturing at UCEM. It is pretty straight to the point, so to help your understanding, I'm adding it here:

Business tenancies in England and Wales are governed by the Landlord and Tenant Act 1954 Part II. Essentially tenancies which fall within this Act have security of tenure. This means they have an automatic right to renew at the end of the lease.

This is incredibly important when looking at commercial investments. Whether a business lease falls within security of tenure (Inside the Act) or not (Outside the Act) will govern the strategy for the investment.

Inside the Act

A business tenancy which falls within the Act, means that the tenant has the right to renew at the end of their lease. A business tenancy will always be inside the act unless it is expressly stated and agreed that it shall be taken outside the act.

Furthermore, a business lease which is Inside the Act does not terminate with the effluxion of time. The tenant is entitled to continue holding over (i.e. in possession of the premises and paying an interim rent) until either the Landlord or Tenant serves notice to terminate, or enter into a new lease, in accordance with the provisions of the Act.

If the Landlord wants to terminate the lease, there are only 7 grounds on which a Landlord can do this:

1. Breach of repairing covenant.
2. Persistent delay in paying rent.
3. Other substantial breach of lease covenants.
4. If the Landlord provides suitable alternative accommodation.
5. Uneconomic subdivision – the Landlord could get more rent from letting the property as a whole.
6. Demolition/reconstruction for development - the Landlord must prove firm intention, prove funding and planning, substantial work and necessity to gain vacant possession.
7. Owner occupation – for re-occupation the Landlord must have owned the premises for 5

years and prove intention to occupy for business purposes.

If the Landlord is successful in ending the lease and agrees on Grounds E to G , the Landlord must pay the tenant compensation. This is 1 x Rateable Value if they have been in occupation for less than 14 years and 2 x Rateable Value if they have been in occupation for over 14 years.

Tip: This is why it is important for landlords to have an active interest in business rates. By keeping business rates low, landlords will have less to pay in compensation if they need to end inside the act lease!

Outside the Act

A business tenancy which is outside the Act does not have the right to renew on expiry of the lease. Therefore, the last day of the lease is the last day of the term. If a new lease isn't agreed then the tenant must vacate.

To agree to a lease outside the Act you must expressly advertise that a lease is outside of the Act. The tenant must also sign a statutory declaration to agree to taking a lease outside of the Act.

You will know if a lease is outside of the Act by reading the lease. It will state that the lease is outside the provisions of section 24-28 of the 1954 Act. These are the sections which govern the right to renew.

Tip: Do not demand or accept rent, service charge, insurance, or any other form of expenditure from a tenant for any period after the expiry of the lease. This might give security of tenure and automatically enter them into a new "inside the act" lease.

Strategy of the 1954 Act

It is important to know whether a business lease is inside or outside the Act. This will govern the strategy around the investment you are buying.

If an inside the Act lease is ending shortly, you may want to wait to purchase the property. The current Landlord can then negotiate vacant possession (VP) and deal with the expense associated with doing this (compensation and legal fees). If it turns out that the current Landlord cannot get VP then you may want to reassess the deal. It may not be worth your time waiting for the next lease to end. This could involve going through the turbulent process of ending the lease. Then if successful, paying the tenant compensation based on current rateable value

However, if you want to retain the current tenant. Consider buying the property quickly and negotiating terms which work for you, rather than letting the current Landlord do it. In this case buy the property prior to the tenant having 12 months left on their lease. Then prepare to serve notice on the tenant for renewal exactly 12 months before the lease ends, the earliest date you can serve notice.

Alternatively, if you are buying a property which you are looking to develop then you will want the business leases to be outside the Act and preferably ending around the same time. What you will notice is that rents are sometimes lower for outside the Act leases. This is because they aren't as tenant friendly.

Tip: Often landlords compensate for lower rents by offering a rent-free period, tenant-only break clause or friendlier rent review clauses. These are all items to look out for and can impact the yield placed on a property.

The Importance of the 1954 Act

Often the 1954 Act isn't a factor taken into consideration by commercial investors. However, it is something that must be understood and discussed with a solicitor.

Prior to getting to the stage of your offer being accepted on a commercial investment, you must decide on your strategy. Then you must look at this in conjunction with the business leases within the building.

If your strategy doesn't work with the lease structures in place you either need to move on to plan B or go and find another property. (Natasha Collins, 2017)

(It was a great blog post, right?)

I've created a free resource detailing how lease renewals of 1954 Act leases work in practice by looking at seven different scenarios. This is an important download as this information will help you put in place a leasing strategy, you can access that by scanning the QR code below:

On the face of it, it looks like the simplest option is to have an Outside the Act Lease because there are no strict procedures to follow and you can get the tenants out at the end of the lease easy-peasy.

Yes, that's correct. This is a really good option if you know you need to get vacant possession at the end of the lease for development purposes or owner-occupation. However, it's not so secure for tenants who want to put down roots in a location.

Tenants would often expect a slight discount in rent for outside the Act leases as opposed to Inside. Again that 5%. Make sure to account for this when looking at what type of lease to put in place.

The other two lease clauses which need detail and can make a significant impact on value are the rent review and break clauses. I've touched on both, but I want to give you a quick run-down on them here and what to look out for. The reason being that whenever there is a lease event this can impact your rental income and therefore you need to understand these lease events to make sure that you can handle and negotiate on the lease event. Usually this is why a surveyor or a solicitor is instructed to oversee the process.

Rent Review

As I've said above, the rent review clause allows you to adjust the rent of your unit at periodic interviews throughout the lease.

At the moment, I'm seeing a lot of Retail Price Index-based (RPI) rent reviews being agreed on, some of which are being capped and collared. Basically, having upper and lower limits so that you know how they are going to work.

More often than not, the RPI rent reviews will be annually and there will be a method of calculation detailed in the lease so that you as the landlord or your managing agent can complete the rent review at the intervals without incurring any costs.

Similarly, your rent review might just stipulate that there are increases of rent to different levels and therefore you can change your rent demands accordingly.

However, where there is an open market rent review, i.e the new market rent has to be determined by the open market, this is tricky to enact and often requires the skills of a surveyor to come and negotiate on your behalf.

You will know if you have an open market rent review clause in your lease because the lease will say that the new rent will be either the Market Rent or the best of the current rent and the Market Rent. Market Rent refers to the current rental value of the property in the open market. It represents the price that a willing landlord and a willing tenant would agree upon for a specific property at a specific time, assuming both parties have reasonable knowledge of the relevant market conditions.

The rent review clause will also include a number of other things which will help in determining the market rent. It will give the hypothetical lease terms, which are the lease terms that the rent has to be valued on. This may or may not correlate with the terms of the actual lease, which is why it usually requires a professional to interpret. Ultimately, if the lease says the hypothetical lease term is for 10 years and for restaurant use only, then that's what you are valuing based on.

Now, if you did your homework and have read the Code for Leasing Business Premises, you will see that generally the hypothetical lease should follow the current lease terms for fairness on both parties. It is wise to check because this could impact your final rental valuation. And, as you have now learnt, if your property isn't being let at market rent then this could severely impact its value.

The other important thing that a rent review clause will say is whether time is of the essence at rent review or not. Time is of the essence refers to whether you must do a rent review by a certain time or not. Usually this is in step with another lease clause, such as a break clause, or it may stipulate that the rent review must be agreed by the rent review date or otherwise there is a certain penalty or the rent review cannot be undertaken. Whatever it says, you must make sure you understand this clause and if time is of the essence (which is increasingly rare) then you are either starting the rent review yourself or handing it over to a professional. Unless you know the market rent has gone down in which case there may be reason to not complete the rent review.

Those are the basic principles. The process of operating an open market rent review will be as follows:

You instruct a surveyor. The surveyor will go out and inspect and measure the property. Then they will establish the Market Rent and make a proposal that the rent review notice should be served at. Please note that the rent at which to serve notice will be higher than where they think the rent will settle, the reason being is that it gives room for negotiation. Once the rent review notice is served on the tenant, the tenant will often instruct their own surveyor and the two surveyors will negotiate and come to an agreement of market rent. This process can take a while–6-12 months! If both sides can't come to an agreement then the lease will provide for a third-party mechanism of either arbitration or independent expert to decide on the rent. Third-party is costly–the last time I went to third party was 2014 (it's rare) and the costs were circa £32,000 on rent of £65,000 per annum, which will either be paid for by the landlord or the tenant or split down the middle depending on what the Arbitrator or Independent expert decides. Again, it is usually in everyone's best interests to keep it as the last option.

Once the new rent is agreed, the tenant signs a rent review memorandum stating that they agree to pay for the new rent from the date of the rent review and they will make any back payments of rent if the rent review was settled after the review date.

The process or open market rent review is lengthy and can also be costly in surveying fees, which is why on smaller properties and rental income most landlords opt for stepped rents or RPI increases.

Again, this process is necessary. You want to keep the rent moving to market rent so that you are always keeping your property value at market value.

Break clauses are important to understand because they are essentially a point in the lease where the tenant can choose to end the lease before the term comes to an end and therefore your rental income stops.

This provision can be designed to align with certain events such as rent review intervals or the landlord's intention to undertake development activities.

The break clause is not always a tenant-only break clause. You can have mutual break clauses where either the landlord or the tenant can break the lease if they enact the trigger, or a landlord-only break clause.

The lease agreement should clearly outline the specific conditions and procedures for the implementation of the break clause. The party breaking the lease must serve the break notice exactly as it states in the lease, otherwise the break is invalid.

In cases where an "Inside the Act" lease is in place, typically only the tenant is allowed to exercise the break clause. However, if there is a mutual or landlord break, the landlord must serve a section 25 notice to initiate the termination process.

It is crucial to understand that break clauses are strictly interpreted by the courts, meaning that even minor errors in the execution of the break can render it invalid. Therefore, if you are a tenant, it is essential to exercise caution when negotiating and utilising a break clause. Careful attention should be given to ensure compliance with all the stipulated requirements.

On the other hand, if you are a landlord, it is prudent to have your solicitors thoroughly review the notice provisions and conditions outlined in the lease before accepting that a tenant's break right has been granted. This ensures that the break clause has been properly implemented and protects the landlord's interests.

The following elements should be carefully considered and fulfilled:

1. The notice must be served by the right tenant. It is essential to identify the specific individual or entity named as the tenant in the lease agreement who has the authority to exercise the break clause. Only the tenant named in the lease has the right to serve the break notice.

2. The notice must be served on the right landlord. Similarly, it is important to identify the correct landlord or landlords as specified in the lease agreement. The break notice should be addressed and delivered to the appropriate party responsible for receiving such notices.

3. The notice should be sent to the right address. The lease agreement should contain the designated address where the break notice must be delivered. It is crucial to ensure that the notice is sent to the correct physical address or, if specified, a specific postbox or email address as stated in the lease agreement.

4. The notice must be served in the proper manner. The lease agreement may specify the acceptable methods of serving the break notice, such as registered mail, hand delivery, or email. It is important to follow the prescribed method to ensure that the notice is legally valid.

5. The correct form should be used. Some lease agreements may require the break notice to be in a specific format or include certain details. It is essential to review the lease agreement and use the appropriate form or template provided, if applicable, to ensure compliance with the contractual requirements.

6. The break notice must be served in good time. The lease agreement will typically specify a specific timeframe within which the break notice must be served. It is crucial to calculate and allow sufficient time for the notice to reach the landlord before the deadline. Late service of the notice may invalidate the exercise of the break clause.

Standard break clauses usually come with three provisions as per the recommendations from the Code of Leasing Business Premises. Those are:

1. The tenant must be up-to-date with the payment of the main rent. This means that all rent payments up until the point of exercising the break clause must be fully paid and not in arrears. If any outstanding rent remains unpaid, the tenant may not be able to utilise the break clause.

2. The tenant is required to give up occupation of the premises. This means that upon exercising the break clause, the tenant must vacate the property and no longer occupy it. The intention behind this condition is to ensure that the termination of the lease is accompanied by the tenant's physical departure from the premises.

3. The break clause often stipulates that no subtenants should be left behind in the property. Sub-tenants are individuals or businesses who have entered into sub-lease agreements with the tenant, leasing a portion of the premises. This condition is typically included to prevent sub-tenants from

claiming rights to a new lease under the provisions of the 1954 Act, which grants security of tenure to certain business tenants.

By including these conditions, the break clause aims to ensure that the tenant has fulfilled their financial obligations, physically vacated the property and that any sub-tenants have left thus preventing them from asserting—their rights under the 1954 Act. These conditions provide safeguards for the landlord, allowing them to regain full control of the property and potentially seek new tenants or pursue other plans for the space.

It is crucial for both tenants and landlords to carefully review and adhere to the specific conditions outlined in the break clause. Failure to meet any of these conditions, even if it is a minor oversight, could invalidate the tenant's right to terminate the lease early. Therefore, tenants should ensure they are compliant with all requirements before exercising the break clause, while landlords should verify that the conditions have been fulfilled before accepting the termination of the lease.

Ultimately, I want you to take away from this chapter that having the right lease in place with a tenant can also help increase the value of the property for you. One thing you should never ever cheap out on is having a good lease drafted by a solicitor. You don't want any ambiguous clauses in there because you could be in a position where during a lease event such as a rent review or a break clause you're arguing with the tenant over what a term or clause means. This can be time-consuming and can also cost you money if you can't agree with the tenant that the clause was written in the way you intended it.

So again, I reiterate, spend money on having a lease put in place for your portfolio and then use it across the board. I'd expect to pay around £1,500 + VAT for a good lease to be drawn up by a solicitor. It's worth your money, I promise. Just think of the value added for getting it done correctly.

The Takeaway

1. The lease is the key document that determines the landlord and tenant relationship.
2. Lease documents help to create property value.
3. Aim for a fair balance within the lease terms – both landlord-focussed and tenant-friendly terms.
4. Understand the requirements of the Landlord and Tenant Act 1954 and remember that there strict timetables for compliance.
5. Rent Reviews and Lease Renewals are part of the regular cycle of business tenancies. Use a chartered surveyor to undertake these.
6. As property managers must comply with the RICS Code of Leasing Business Premises, you should too.

13

Finding the Right Commercial Tenant

Now that we've discussed putting in place leases, what about actually finding a tenant who's going to take the lease that you want to put in place?

Before we get going on how to actually find these tenants, you may, like most other commercial investors, be fretting about finding tenants.

I've never had a property stand empty forever. There are always tenants to be found. However, you should be doing research into the type of tenant that is going to take your space. Here's what you can do:

1. Check with local agents, find out how long things are taking to let and what kind of tenants you can expect to get in your space.

2. Look at stats on industry portals such as CoStar, which give you an indication as to how long units like yours are taking to let.

3. Go to your local Chamber of Commerce. Speak to local businesses in the area, see what kind of space they are looking to take up.

4. Do a Google street view of the local area and identify gaps in the market for certain types of tenants. When you see that gap in the market you can then approach that tenant by typing in on Google, 'The estate department for____' and then in that space, type the commercial tenant that you are looking to attract. Or you could go on LinkedIn and search for either the Acquisitions manager or the Estates manager for the tenant that you are looking to find. Finally, you can simply Google the potential tenant and see if they've got contact details for their head office and give them a call directly. There is no harm in doing this. You may be presenting them

with an opportunity that they did not know about and they may be desperate for a space like yours. The worst the potential tenant can say is 'no'.

5. Join business Facebook groups and connect with local business owners and see what space they would like.

6. Use Requirements List, an online tool, which tells you which tenants are looking for space in your area.

7. You can use CoStar to identify which tenant's leases are coming to an end soon and you can then reach out to the tenants directly to see if they would be interested in moving into your building when their current lease comes to an end.

With reaching out to tenants prior to having a vacant space actually ready or if you've not yet purchased the building, be wary that the tenant doesn't go out and look at the opportunity themselves. You need to make sure that you keep discretion when discussing a soon-to-be purchased commercial unit with a potential tenant.

If none of this satisfies you then you can take matters into your own hands and run adverts to the community around your building and see who would be interested in joining your space. I've seen landlords have great success with creating a Facebook page for the building. You can use AI Tools like Runway to create an image for you of the building. From there you can create a waiting list form which potential tenants can fill in to say they are interested in taking the space. You can then run ads to your waiting list form, targeted at entrepreneurs in the local area and see who is interested in taking a space.

Using all of this research you can test the water and see what types of tenants are going to want your space, and by doing this you will probably find that you'll get some interest in the building and could do some pre-letting. We've been through what happens when you are looking for demand. Say you've got a building with space to let, what are you going to do?

I'm a firm believer of a two-pronged approach when you are going out to find commercial tenants. Of course, the standard approach that we know is putting the property on the market with a local commercial agent and letting them list the property on local search portals such as property link by Estates Gazette, Loop Net or

Rightmove. It's preferable to hire an agent because they know how to market the property correctly. For example, you could put a marketing board in the window or on the side of the property. They could use marketing flyers or brochures which detail the specifics of a property. An agent would also have a list of people and tenants in the local area who may be searching for a commercial property; they would have details of other agents who are acting for tenants who are actively looking in the local market. Agents may also be able to host professional events or use Innovative Marketing Solutions such as vinyl displays in Windows or other Solutions in order to attract tenants into your unit.

For this type of service, you could expect to pay roughly 10% of the first year's rent.

This is the standard way of finding a tenant. It could happen quickly or it could take time. The key thing you need to remember is that whilst a unit is empty it is going to cost you money-for business rates if the short Empty Business Rates Relief period has expired. It will also cost you money in maintenance costs because you will need to pick up the percentage that the commercial unit should be paying towards the maintenance costs for the period that the property is empty. Furthermore, you may also need to pay the rebuilding insurance premium and for additional security to stop any trespassers from getting into your empty commercial unit.

This is why you need prong 2 of this approach. You need to be going out there and finding commercial tenants and approaching the right tenants. To do this you're going to need to get creative. As you will have seen from doing your demand study, it's important that you do research into the local area to find out what commercial tenants are already doing really well and whether the local area has gaps in the market for certain types of tenants.

From your demand study you may also have a list of tenants at your fingertips who are ready to enter into a new lease. You should be reaching out to them as soon as you know you have a space available and asking them to take a lease with you. If they show interest at that point, you can give them the marketing details from the agent or the details that you put together for the least that you wanted to get and they can then analyse that and see if it works for them. Remember here that if the tenant shows even a little bit of interest to follow up every single week to see if it's still something that they would like to look at until the point they say no.

The Lease You Are Marketing

I've mentioned above that you need to give the tenant marketing details. Within that you need to include what you are looking for from the lease, so include the length of a term that you are willing to offer, whether it is inside the act or outside the act and how much rent you are looking for. This way the tenant will know what to expect when they enter into negotiations for you.

You will need to either go out and do your research in the market (which I have already discussed at length that you should do) as to what the rent should be or you will need to discuss this with your agent. A good marketing tactic is to put the rent slightly higher than you would expect to get on the market so as to give you room to negotiate with a potential tenant. You can always put in the marketing details that the rent is open to offers. Once you've been out to the market and you've gone and sought out tenants, or tenants have come to you, they will have a look around the unit, do an analysis as to whether this will work for them and their business, and then they will come to you with an offer. When you are looking at tenants' offers, it's not just the amount of rent that they've offered you that you should be looking at.

Remember, the value of a commercial property does come from the amount of rent because you are going to be looking at getting market rent, but it also comes from the security that a tenant will offer when entering into the lease and taking occupation.

Concessions for Taking a Lease

It is usual practice for a landlord to offer a tenant concessions to take a lease on a premises. This is the sweetener to incentivise the tenant to come in, fit out the unit to their own brand style and put down roots so that they want to stay for a long period of time.

You can choose what concessions to offer and your agent will also advise you on this, but here are a few options:

1. A rent-free period. The standard is 3 months (more is given in a tough commercial market).

2. A capital contribution to the tenant's fit-out cost.

3. The rental deposit to be paid over a number of months. For example, if it is a 3-month deposit, a third is paid in month 1, a third in month two and the final third in month three to help the tenant with cash flow.

4. The landlord could do works before the tenants takes occupation.

5. Anything else you can think of that will help the tenant with their business.

Be creative, but again this is meant to help support the tenant so that they can build their business from your property.

Analysing a Tenant's Offer

Once you've started marketing the unit, you should pretty soon start to see tenants coming in with an offer to take a lease on your unit.

I'm going to go through the six key things that you need to look at when analysing tenants' offers so that you can maximise the value of your property and you can also make sure that you are getting the best tenant.

Amount of Rent

The first thing that you need to look at is of course the amount of rent. You need to look at how much the tenant is offering you. Is this in line with local market rents? And is this what you wanted as part of your portfolio strategy?

Tenants Ability to Pay and Covenant Strength

Secondly, you need to look at the tenant's ability to pay. Can that tenant actually pay the rent agreed? Now, this will require you looking at the tenant's covenant strength. This is the financial strength of the tenant leasing a property. And to do that you are going to be looking at their financial history, so you're going to be looking at the last three years accounts. You will also need to see if you can obtain a reference from the previous landlord or even the bank of the tenant. A tenant's covenant strength can also be seen by how many other locations they have. For example, H&M is a very strong covenant and operates on a global scale. Therefore, if one of their stores was not making a profit, they would be able to cover this from other stores' profits. However, if you are leasing to a tenant that is a startup, or maybe doesn't have much trading history or any other stores/offices/similar premises which could pay for any rent service charge or business rates that they can't afford, this may suggest that they are a weaker covenant.

Now, there are things that you can put in place to protect yourself as a landlord. For example, you can have a large deposit. You can take anywhere between a 3 and 12-month rental deposit, or you can ask for a personal guarantee from the tenant. To do that, you will need to check if the tenant has a number of assets that would be worth pursuing in the event that they didn't pay the rent. These are things that you can think about in order to increase the tenant's covenant strengths because you as a landlord have that fallback option. But this goes back to the original point. If a tenant cannot pay the rent that they are offering, you do not want them in the unit. Therefore, you definitely need to check a tenant's ability to pay and their covenant strength. So those are the two things that you need to check in order to see whether they would be financially able to cover the rent, the service charge and the business rates on the unit for the length of the term of the lease that they are proposing.

Lease Terms

Next up, number four, you need to be checking the lease terms that the tenant wants to take. This is a really good estate management strategy. The reason being is that you will want all of the leases in your building to fall in line with one another. That's because at the end of the lease that gives you the option to do what you would like. The caveat is that you would have an "Outside the Act" lease so that all leases, when they come to the end, it is up to you to renegotiate. However, if you have an "Inside the Act" lease, it may be that you're not so concerned with all of the leases ending at the same date, as the tenant will have the right to renew and therefore chances are that they will look to extend or assign to lease to a tenant who wants the right to renew. Other things that you need to look at are rent review patterns, which means what years the rent reviews are going to be in. Ideally, you would have a rent review every three to five years which raised the rent in line with market rents at the time, but you could also choose to have a stepped rent. So year one it was £10,000. Year two it's £11,000. Year three it's £12,000, and so on. Or you could have your rent increase with RPI or CPI, depending on what you think is going to be best for you and your property circumstance.

Again, I reiterate that the value of this property comes from the rental value and the rental income. So if you can maximise that throughout the term of the lease, you are maximising the value of the property. You also need to be looking at break clauses. A tenant-only break clause is valuable to the tenant. Whereas if you have a landlord-only break clause, that's valuable for you so long as you want the right to develop or for whatever reason you may need the right to ask the tenant to leave their premises.

If you've got a mutual break clause it gives you both the right to end the lease at the specified time within the lease. Now, if you offer a tenant-only break clause because the tenant is insistent on it, to give value to you, you may want to put in place a break premium whereby the tenant has to pay you a certain amount of money if they leave. That then makes the break valuable for you and it puts a penalty on the tenant, which could stop them from wanting to enact the break. These clauses are really important because, again, remember that the way to maximise the value of this property is to have your tenant pay market rent for the longest period of time, so you want to consider your leased clauses to make sure that that's the strategy you are taking.

Use Class

Next up, you're going to look at the use of the property. Your commercial premises will be designated with a use class that the premises can be used for. For example, A1 is retail, A3 is restaurant use, A5 is takeaways. Maybe it's designated B1 office use. Whatever the designation is, you need to look into that to make sure that you are attracting the right tenants. It may be that the tenant could get their own change of use. That would be up to them to do if you are allowing that to happen. Just be aware that if that tenant doesn't get that change of use, they may try and give you the keys back to that premises so it really is worth your while doing your due diligence to make sure that the tenant can use the premises for what they want to use the premises for and then you put that use into the lease.

Tenant Mix

Finally, it's very important that you look at the tenant mix. Tenant mix seeks to balance complementary occupiers in a building or neighbouring units. A good tenant mix will give each tenant the ability to maximise on their profits and captivate a local audience whilst fitting in with other traders in the immediate location. Such a mix creates harmony.

Ideally, you would have a clear tenant mix policy and this would say what tenant type you are looking for. Maybe, if there is already a Chinese restaurant and an Indian restaurant on the street that you're looking at, you would want an Italian restaurant or maybe a pizza shop. Similarly, if there are already three estate agents on the street where you've got a retail unit, you might not want to accept another estate agent into your unit. You have to make sure that you're balancing out competition.

Now, there are places where having the same tenant type is really beneficial. If you have been to Kings Road in

Southwest London, at one end of Kings Road is an area called the Chelsea Design Quarter. In that area, there are loads of designers who have different interior design shops, for example, beds, antiques, clocks, paintings. Having that group of retailers together is really beneficial because people and consumers go to that area specifically to shop for those types of things, so it makes it very user friendly.

Conversely, if you look at a pizza shop with residential tenants above, this might not be a good tenant mix because the pizza shop might be extracting bad fumes, it might be noisy or there might be grease going off into the residential units, which is going to mean that you're going to have some very upset residential tenants. You don't want this because it will be so tough to manage and you will end up losing tenants because they won't want to live or trade there.

Have a think about large shopping centres where certain types of tenants are clustered together, for example, high-end retail versus the low-end retailers. Usually in the middle you have restaurants and then you have leisure use such as cinemas or gyms. Centres are laid out this way to promote footfall and dwell time so that you are captivating the shoppers in the area so that they use all of the different tenants. Whilst you may think that you are a small landlord and you only have one or two units, your careful consideration about tenant mix can make a large difference because you are thinking about your tenant and whether they will fit in. If they don't fit in, you will lose a tenant quickly because they won't trade and therefore won't be able to pay the rent.

So what can you do? You can't use Street View or even get out on foot and wander up around the local area and see what types of tenants are needed so that you can have a good idea of what tenant would fit in. This is the same for office, this is the same for industrial, this is the same for retail, and even in mixed use buildings, this applies. You want to have tenants that are a balance of trades, they complement one another, and ultimately, they don't annoy each other, because annoyed tenants aren't going to want to stick around. Tenant mix can actually be one of the most important factors when selecting a tenant, because ultimately, a good tenant mix is going to be what keeps your tenant in a unit.

Those are the six things that you need to analyse when looking at tenant's offers. Once you've analysed offers and selected the appropriate tenant, you can still go back to that tenant with a counter-offer. Maybe the lease terms don't work, or maybe the rent's slightly too low. You could present the tenants with a counter-offer, agree on a compromise and then set out the heads of terms accordingly. *That* is how you find the right tenant.

What you should have grasped from this chapter is that you need to be proactive in finding tenants. If you aren't doing this yourself, then you need to engage with agents who are going to be proactive in finding you tenants. Your agents should be checking in with you weekly, telling you about the level of interest that you've had and what the feedback is from tenants so that you can make decisions on whether it's best to change your marketing tactics, alter the rent or maybe upgrade the property in some way in order to attract better tenants. You could even add this into your terms of business when you agree to it with the agent so that they know to do this every week, since it's a contractual obligation.

Ultimately, the sooner you get a tenant into your vacant unit, the less it costs you.

The Takeaway

1. Thorough research of the local market is critical. Use the various online portals, social media sites and personal contact.

2. Unlet buildings will cost you more than a lack of rental income. You will need to ensure the property is fully covered with rebuilding insurance, pay business rates that might be reduced, pay for increased security measures and be responsible for any repairs or damage that occur.

3. Be prepared to offer incentives and concessions to encourage tenants such as a rent-free fit-out period, capital contribution toward fit-out or a stepped rent pattern.

4. Carefully analyse any and all potential tenants.

14

Risk Management

If you haven't guessed it by now, investing in commercial property is risky. After all, the value of commercial property depends on its risk level.

At the time of writing, May 2024, you can get a circa 5% interest rate on your savings in a bank. However, when you net down your commercial property income (rental income minus mortgage and expenses), you may not actually be yielding 5%.

In practice, this is acceptable due to the heavily inflationary times we find ourselves in. If you had purchased your property anytime in the two years prior, a 6.5% net yield on a property investment would have been seen as fabulous. Unfortunately, interest rates on mortgages have risen, which has not helped the net yields. Chances are, you are making less than what you could be getting from a bank.

But property investment is a long-term game. Over an extended period, you are more likely to average a 4% net yield. This is steadier than the fluctuations from 0.1% to 6.5% in a bank, which could ultimately average out to a lower yield over your investment's time frame.

The central question of this chapter is 'How do you manage risk?'

Determining Your Risk Tolerance

Firstly, you need to decide how much risk you are prepared to take on. In the world of commercial property, the general rule is simple:

- The higher the yield, the higher the risk.
- The lower the yield, the lower the risk.

For instance, a 3.5% yield is considered the lowest risk. You are likely to maintain this income from a property into perpetuity. On the other hand, yields of 10%-12% are riskier, indicating that you may only receive the current income for a short period before potentially facing a lower rent, a prolonged void period or a number of tenants not paying rent.

Many investments come to auction with an enticing 14% yield or higher. Sounds incredible, right? On the surface it is an incredible yield, but usually the deal has problems.

Conduct an analysis of the market rent, and you may find that the rent in the area has dropped significantly since the last review or lease renewal. Alternatively, the rent that is quoted to get to that high yield may be the headline rent. But tenants not paying the rent or who are about to move out will mean that you lose rental income and the yield won't look so good.

One of my clients recently purchased a property on the Isle of Wight. The deal looked tasty. At the auction it was advertised at a guide price of £750,000 with an income of £96,100 per annum, which is a 12.81% yield. It had run at auction twice and not sold. When we analysed the deal, we realised that a number of tenants had stopped paying and therefore my client could only rely on £61,300 per annum coming in. After much negotiating, we ended up purchasing the property for £625,000 (a 15.38% yield when fully let and all tenants paying), on the basis that we knew we had to sort out non-paying tenants and pull the management back in line.

Here are another three deals that completed at different yield rates:

The first is a fully let deal in Chippenham. The purchase price was acquired for £135,000 at a 8.15% yield. Despite a five-month process due to documentation exchanges, the property offered stability with a long term lease and a single tenant responsible for internal repairs. The purpose of this deal was to pop it in my clients SSAS to provide consistent income.

Another deal to compare this to is a building another client purchased in Burton-on-Trent. With a yield of 9.65%, this property, acquired for £228.000 with a £22,000 income, assured stable returns. This deal had a prolonged completion period, attributed to lease renegotiations and property repairs which the seller had agreed to get done before completion, as it spreads risk with two commercial tenants. However, one of the leases only had less than a year left to run, hence the higher yield. On purchase, my client extended this for 5 years, again making it a great SSAS purchase. Please note that the client did know that the tenant wanted to extend their lease prior to buying as they talked to the tenant on viewing!

In Dereham, my client purchased a building for £167,000, at an 11% yield. Featuring a retail unit and two offices, its prime location and tenant interest underscored its potential for long-term returns. This was an auction property, but it didn't sell initially. The reason being that it had a lot of maintenance problems and the anchor tenant was 'unstable', meaning they wanted to leave, which they did 4 weeks after purchase. Luckily, it was purchased at a high yield so a decent income is still coming in whilst our client looks for new tenants.

You can see from these examples how the lower the yield, the more stable the income. On the other hand, the higher the yield, the more risky the income.

Choose your yield wisely based on your actual risk appetite. If you're comfortable with developments or tenant changes that could lead to substantial gains but also potential losses, then aim for those double-digit yields. However, always conduct sensitivity analyses to understand the impact of variations in your predictions. Can you live with the potential outcomes?

Compare this to a building where you buy and hold, collecting rent and managing minimal responsibilities. It may offer a 9% yield but consider how far this is from your higher-yielding property if it underperforms.

The key point here is that the level of risk is a personal decision. Do not be swayed by others' opinions. Continually evaluate your risk tolerance as part of your investment strategy. Pick a percentage you'd like to get as a return and go for it.

The Tale of Two Property Markets

Interestingly, there seems to be a split in the commercial property sector, divided by purchase price:

Sub-£500,000 purchases are seeing lower yields as more cash flows into this market segment. A medium-risk property may be sold at around 7%, compared to the traditional 8%, 9%, or even 10%. Mortgage interest rates are not dropping much lower than 8.5%.

In the £800,000 plus arena, yields are higher. Low-risk properties are being sold at 8% or 9% yields, with interest rates for properties at this level tumbling below 7%. This is because there are fewer market players at this level, and banks perceive larger properties as less risky, providing better returns for investors.

Therefore your budget for your commercial property purchase may also influence the yield you pick.

Why Balancing Risk in Your Portfolio is a Must

At any given moment, multiple trends are changing, affecting the commercial property landscape:

- Base and interest rates have risen dramatically since late 2022, altering lending costs and accessibility.
- Government legislation changes, such as EPC regulations, health and safety requirements, and The Renters (Reform) Bill 2023, are reshaping the landlord-tenant relationship.
- Economic changes, including inflation and tightening budgets, have led to rising interest rates.
- Cultural and social shifts influence spending habits.

Change is constant, which is why balancing your portfolio is crucial. You have to understand which way it's changing and consider risks related to location, property type, market conditions and regulatory factors. Is the economy going to get worse? Does that mean the base rate is going to go up even further? Will that impact interest rates? Ultimately, when there is less money in circulation and it costs more to borrow money, there is less demand. Combine that with my earlier statement about investors being able to get good returns in a bank right now and you've got a lack of demand in a market. Also, where market players are worried about the economy because the news and every media outlet is spinning stories about it, they are more likely to keep their money in their pocket. Again, resulting in less demand. In return this will cause the market to stagnant or fall as transactions are going through at lower prices or they just aren't happening.

Diversification is the key to smoothing out price fluctuations across your entire investment portfolio. In commercial property, diversification means more than just investing in one use class or area. It involves careful consideration of various factors, including property type, location and yield.

Risk Assessment

Now that the introduction to risk management is out of the way, how are you going to assess the risk?

In the context of commercial property investment in the UK, risks can be broadly categorised into internal and external risks, each with its own set of factors and considerations. Here's an explanation of both types of risks:

1. Internal Risks

Internal risks are those that are within the control or influence of the property owner or investor. They often relate to decisions, actions, or conditions specific to the property or the investment itself. Internal risks include:

- **Property Management Risks**

  These are associated with the day-to-day management of the property. Common property management risks include:

  - Tenant turnover and vacancy rates
  - Maintenance and repair issues
  - Property security and safety concerns
  - Compliance with local regulations and zoning laws

- **Financial Risks**

  Financial risks are related to the economic aspects of property investment and can include:

- Rent collection and tenant default
- Property valuation fluctuations
- Financing and interest rate risks
- Capital expenditure and budgeting challenges

- **Tenant Risks**

  The choice of tenants can significantly impact investment outcomes. Tenant-related risks may include:

  - Lease negotiations and terms
  - Tenant creditworthiness and stability
  - Lease renewal and rent escalations
  - Tenant industry-specific risks (e.g., retail industry trends)

- **Operational Risks**

  These risks encompass various operational aspects of the property, such as:

  - Efficiency of property management
  - Effective marketing and advertising to attract tenants

- Utility and maintenance costs
- Energy efficiency and sustainability measures

- **Legal and Regulatory Risks**

  Compliance with laws and regulations is crucial in property investment. These risks include:

  - Use class changes or restrictions
  - Environmental regulations and liability
  - Tenant disputes and legal actions
  - Contractual obligations and obligations to third parties

2. External Risks

External risks are beyond the control of the property owner or investor and often result from external factors or market conditions. These risks can impact the overall performance of the investment and may include:

- **Market Risks**

  Market conditions can fluctuate and affect property values, rental rates, and demand for commercial spaces. Market risks include:

- Economic downturns and recessions
- Changes in supply and demand for commercial real estate
- Interest rate fluctuations
- Competition from new developments

- **Political and Regulatory Risks**

  Government policies and regulations can impact property investments. Examples include changes in tax laws, zoning regulations, and rent control ordinances.

- **Environmental Risks**

  Natural disasters, climate change, and environmental hazards can pose external risks. These may include floods, hurricanes, earthquakes, or pollution concerns.

- **Geographic and Location Risks**

  The physical location of a property can introduce risks such as exposure to crime, changes in neighbourhood dynamics, or transportation infrastructure changes.

- **Global and Regional Economic Factors**

  Economic conditions at both global and regional levels, including inflation, currency fluctuations, and trade policies, can influence commercial property investment.

To assess these risks, use a SWOT analysis. We covered this when searching for a property and finding the right location. This is a risk assessment. Understanding the strengths, weaknesses, opportunities and threats of an area is important. It's equally important to do it for each of the properties you are looking at.

You have to understand the way the market is moving, because you don't want to buy, the market drops some more and then you try to sell. Not a good idea.

Instead, you want to make sure that even if you are buying in a falling market, you can keep hold of that property plus make some money until the market picks back up again and you're at a place for selling for profit.

At this point, I hear the hecklers at the back saying, 'Why would anyone sell in this market?!' Either they've been forced or they've made their money and are happy to get out because it is tax efficient for them or they want to use their money elsewhere. Ultimately, whilst it is good to know why someone is selling their property so that you can use it as a negotiation tactic, it's not for you to get into a seller's head and decide for them whether they should be buying or selling at this point in time.

Stay in your lane, do your own risk assessment and decide whether the risk in an area and a property hits your target investment goals. Make sure that you are confident that the strengths and opportunities identified within your SWOT analysis outweigh the weaknesses and threats.

Risk Tolerance and Risk Appetite Quiz

I've explored a lot of elements of risk and how you mitigate against it. I also suggested that you figure out your risk tolerance and what yield works for you.

If you don't have a number, I've created a quiz whereby you answer each of the questions with a number from 3 to 10, where 3 is low tolerance for risk and 10 is high tolerance for risk. Why start with 3? This is because 3 is the lowest yield I've seen on commercial properties and therefore the least risky yield in commercial property.

Here are the questions:

1. On a scale of 3 to 10, how comfortable are you with the idea of investing in properties with potential for higher returns but also higher associated risks?

2. When it comes to vacancy risk, where 3 represents a strong preference for stable, long-term tenants and 10 signifies a willingness to take on more turnover, where do you fall on the scale?

3. Regarding leverage and financing, where 3 indicates a preference for low debt and 10 indicates a willingness to use significant leverage, where does your risk tolerance lie?

5. How do you rate your appetite for market risk, with 3 being a preference for stable, established markets and 10 representing a willingness to invest in emerging or volatile markets?

6. On a scale of 3 to 10, how open are you to investing in property types with more significant regulatory and compliance risks, such as historic buildings or environmentally sensitive properties?

7. In terms of tenant quality and credit risk, where 3 signifies a strong preference for blue-chip tenants and 10 implies a willingness to work with startups and smaller businesses, where do you position yourself?

8. When considering development or redevelopment projects, how would you rate your comfort with construction and project risk, with 3 being risk-averse and 10 being highly risk-tolerant?

9. On the risk-return spectrum, where 3 indicates a primary focus on capital preservation and 10 represents a primary focus on maximising returns, where do your investment goals fall?

10. Regarding exit strategy, where 3 represents a preference for long-term, stable investments and 10 indicates a willingness to pursue shorter-term,

potentially higher-risk opportunities, where do you stand?

11. How would you rate your overall risk tolerance for commercial property investment, with 3 being low tolerance and 10 being high tolerance, when considering various factors collectively?

Once you've completed all of the questions add up each of the numbers. Once you've got a total, divide it by 10. That is the overall yield you should be aiming for in your portfolio based on your risk appetite.

The Takeaway

1. Investment in commercial property is risky, and that's why the rewards can be high.
2. Remember that commercial property is for the long-term.
3. Set your risk appetite and tolerances: initial budget, finance rate and yield requirement.
4. Recognise the impact of external influences such as global economics, national political landscape,

legislative change, lending costs and shifts in consumer spending.

5. Recognise the internal risks associated with the property such as tenant issues, structure and materials and legislation.

6. Use both SWOT analysis and the Quiz to help clarify your thoughts and set your parameters.

15

Insurance

In this section, I want to talk to you about insurance, and specifically rebuilding insurance.

Now, insurance is really important because building insurance mitigates against any loss caused by accidental damage to your building. If something happens, for example, an act of God or a leak or an awful storm, then your insurance should cover you for loss of rent if the tenant can no longer trade. In this case, your insurance will pay for the rebuilding of the building if it falls down and it will also provide alternative accommodation for the tenant so that they can go and trade for somewhere else if they need to. Finally, your insurance should also cover you for any acts of terrorism.

As a commercial landlord, your responsibility is to take it out. The tenant's lease will state whether the tenant should pay the insurance premium. For the most part, the tenant should pay unless they are on all-inclusive rent, such as serviced offices.

I want to go back to rebuilding the building if it falls down. This means if the building gets completely destroyed, the insurance will cover the full cost of rebuilding it. It is so important that you insure the building for an appropriate amount to have the building fully reinstated.

If you don't, you as the landlord would have to pay for the difference between what the insurance will pay out and what the actual cost of rebuilding the building is.

How do you analyse what the reinstatement cost should be? Well, the first way would be to get a reinstatement cost assessment from a building surveyor. Essentially, you get in contact with your local building surveyor and you ask them for a quote for putting together a reinstatement cost assessment. The building surveyor will come out and measure your building. They will look at how much the cost will be on a £ per metre squared basis to rebuild your building from the ground up. Then, they will multiply that £ per metre squared by the size of your building to get a reinstatement cost value. The sum of that is the full amount that it would cost to rebuild the building.

It is a very good idea to have the building cost assessment undertaken every three to five years. The reason being is that it costs change. In the interim period, annual building cost inflation can be taken into account by the insurance company. And again, I reiterate, you do not want to be underinsured here. It will not be of any use to you should that building fall down. And whilst you may say, 'Natasha, it's not likely that the building is going to fall down,' that probably means that at some point your building will fall down because that is the way luck works. So make sure that you're properly insured.

You must tell your insurer if the building becomes vacant or you're going to do a redevelopment, as the insurer will want to update their policy. They will give you a set of guidelines to follow to make sure your building stays insured during this period. Follow the guidelines.

When you're taking out an insurance policy, your insurer will ask for all of the details of the leases, what the tenants do, how long they're going to be in there, how much rent they're paying. This is because they need to make sure that they get appropriate cover for you. There are also some tenants that are more risky than others. Hairdressers, for example, because they may have chemicals, are seen as more risky. Places that cook hot food are seen as more risky. Storage that's not checked on regularly is seen as more risky as there could be combustible items in there that could cause the building to burn down.

When you get your rebuilding insurance premium quote, your insurer should tell you how much they've allocated to each part of the premises. If there is a part of the premises which is deemed more risky, you can charge that tenant more of the insurance premium based upon what they do.

The existing lease will tell you whether you can charge for buildings insurance and when you can charge for it. Here you can charge for the insurance based upon service charge percentages or the area that the tenant occupies within the building. Pro-rata accordingly and charge the tenants.

Now let's look at making a claim. The excess on any claim will be covered by the service charge or the tenants in the building if they're responsible for paying the building insurance.

The excess is not a landlord's expense unless it's an all-inclusive lease and the landlord is responsible to pay the building's insurance. If any event happens whereby there may need to be a claim on the insurance, call the insurer and notify them that there might be a claim.

If you decide not to make a claim, let the insurer know that's not going to be a mark on your policy. If you do decide to make a claim, follow the directions of your insurer who will tell you what to do.

Make sure that you are claiming appropriately. Get a cost for the works that you are claiming for, and be sensible in whether you should make the claim or not. For example, if your excess is £500 and the cost of work is £600, you might think we're just going to pay for the cost of work rather than go through the insurance claim, which may make my insurance premium higher next year and cost the tenants more money.

It's a really good idea in this instance to consult the tenants and give them the options of either claiming on the insurance or doing the work through the service charge. What you could say is that a numerical majority vote will win and give the results of the vote to the tenants and then do what they have mandated. This is a really transparent way of making that decision. Obviously, if the tenants aren't interested, you can make the decision for them.

Speaking of tenants, tenants need to have their own contents insured. There should be an express clause in the lease requiring tenants to have contents insurance. Make sure to give your tenants a nudge about this, because sometimes tenants forget and then get cross if any of their possessions get damaged and they aren't insured. The rebuilding insurance cover will not include their contents. However, if they do have contents insurance and their contents are damaged by a problem with the structure of the building, for example, a leak, you can put the tenant's contents insurer in contact with the building's insurance and they'll deal with each other accordingly.

Now, to reiterate, as the landlord, when it comes to insurance, your only responsibility is to look after the building and make sure your building is correctly insured.

What I recommend is that every time your policy comes up for renewal, you go out and get three quotes and see which is the most competitive quote. The other option is, if you are a landlord with multiple properties, you could see about getting a portfolio policy and whether this will be cheaper. When you do get a portfolio policy, your insurer will tell you how much of the insurance premium is allocated to each of the properties, so you know how to invoice accordingly.

Just remember, keep that building insured properly, so that in the event that you need to make a claim, you know that you can recover all of the costs associated with the necessary works. That keeps you happy and that keeps the tenants happy.

The Takeaway

1. Full rebuilding insurance is absolutely essential especially if you are borrowing money to fund the purchase.

2. The building reinsurance insurance market is very competitive but you must be prudent in your selection of company. Consider three quotes at every renewal.

3. Ensure that the rebuilding insurance covers terrorism, loss of income, the full cost of relocation of existing tenants.

4. Ensure that the property's external dimensions are correct as they will be used to calculate the rebuilding cost.

5. In single-let buildings under a Full Insuring and Repairing lease, the tenant is responsible for ensuring the building is kept insured. A prudent landlord will require to see the policy and evidence that the premium has been paid.

6. In multi-let buildings, the insurance will be a service charge item and the landlord is responsible for paying the premium.

7. Tenants are responsible for paying a separate insurance premium for their own business-related goods.

16

Exit Strategies

I know at this point in the book, I have shown you exactly how to invest in commercial property, how to go out there and get it done and make sure that you are buying something that actually suits your goals.

Now, at this stage, we're going to talk about exit strategies. And I realise that you might think, 'Natasha, no way. There is no way I'm selling these properties that I have worked so hard to build up to increase the value on. Why on earth would I want to sell?' That is a phenomenal question.

So the main reasons why you may want to exit are number one, if you have done everything you can to a property. You have increased the length of the leases, you have put in place really great tenants, you have made sure that the property is managed really well. You have put in place a good service charge that is maintaining the building. The building is sustainable, or at least it's not overly expensive from a utility point of view, for those tenants to pay for.

If you have done all of that and you're somewhere near the top of the market, where yields are looking really good, prime yields are looking really good, you can check again those prime yield guides to see how the market is looking. If the market is on an up, you will find that there are a lot of investors who want to look at buying commercial property because it will be in a boom stage. So if you are in that situation, it would be worth getting the property valued, seeing how much of an increase you have made on it, and having a look and seeing whether the money that you got from selling that property could be used better somewhere else.

Could you reuse that money for another opportunity? And if you've got more money, that means that you can buy a bigger building that has similar characteristics to the building that you've just bought. And you can go through the cycle again. Improving the covenant of the tenants, making sure that the leases are great, making sure that you're getting good market rent in, making sure that the building has a good service charge and is well maintained. You increase the value of that building, you sell it and then you go for a bigger building. That is how all the big investors end up getting to buy huge property portfolios because they just keep increasing and increasing and increasing. When they cannot do any more for a property, they sell it, they take the money out because there's always going to be investors who are going to want to invest in a low-risk opportunity that's just going to pay out because it has been put into such a good condition.

So that would be the first reason that you want to exit. Essentially, you've done everything you can for the building and now you are looking for a better opportunity and a better place to put your money.

The next reason you might want to exit is similar to the first, maybe over the hold period of your building. You have got all of your money back out of it and more because you've been holding for 10, 20, 30 years and you want to go and do something else with the money, in which case you would sell. And that's a personal decision.

Reason number 3 may be because the building has become a headache. It is not something you enjoy running anymore. The tenants aren't being easy. Maybe you've just absolutely had enough of the building. And for some investors, that's where they get to. They don't want to deal with that building anymore. That's OK. What you need to do is make sure that you've actually made some money out of this building. So again, you want to forecast your income and your expenditure and make sure that you've made a profit on the building and then price the building accordingly and put it on the market to sell.

Finally, it may be because the building is either not letting or it's costing you too much to maintain and you need to cut your losses. There are occasions where you buy a building, you use it for its lifecycle and find that building has run its course. It's no longer in demand. There's no longer anybody who wants to use it for its particular use. And you don't have the finances to go and do up that building or put it back into a usable condition.

If that is you, you may decide to sell because ultimately you can take the money out and put it elsewhere. It's all about what the money in that building could do for you if it was put elsewhere. That is why you would exit out of commercial property.

A tip that I would offer is when you are looking at exiting or selling your property, you should have a look at whether you can group properties together and sell as a portfolio. This might be attractive for a larger investor who wants to buy a collection of properties. If you are selling a company with commercial properties in it, there are advantages to the purchaser because they might not have to pay Stamp Duty Land Tax. So there are reasons why you would sell properties together and you would commission a portfolio valuation. If that whole portfolio is pretty risk-free and has been managed and maintained well, chances are you will get a really good price for it.

The other thing that you can do is have a look and see if you would get more money by selling off parts of a property. For example, if you have got a mixed-use property such as a residential flat above and the commercial unit on the ground floor, you may want to sell the residential element and the commercial element separately and achieve more money than you would get if you were to sell the building as a whole on investment value. Whenever you are looking at selling, please make sure that you get an appraisal on whether the building should be sold as a whole or whether the building should be sold in parts. And speaking to a couple of different agents or even getting a professional valuation done (which is going to cost you a couple of thousand pounds maximum), is probably a very good use of your money so that you can make the most when you dispose.

For those of you who have bought in cash, an exit strategy could be seen as remortgaging and pulling capital out of a property. Then you can use that money elsewhere. I tend to see exit strategies of completely disposing of a property and not holding it anymore. But of course, if you've bought in cash, that is an option for you.

The Takeaway

1. For some, the end of the journey.
2. Disposal is part of the bigger cycle.
3. There are different reasons to sell. Ensure that the reasons and timing are right for you.
4. Sell as an individual unit, a portfolio or consider separate sales of commercial and residential elements.
5. An exit strategy should be a part of your larger investment strategy.

References

Bath and North East Somerset Council. (2023). New Business Openings in Bath City Centre. [Online] Available at: https://newsroom.bathnes.gov.uk/news/new-business-openings-bath-city-centre (Accessed: 7 May 2023).

Bath and North East Somerset Council. (2022). Planning Application Details: Reference 22/02352/FUL. [Online] Available at: https://www.bathnes.gov.uk/webforms/planning/details .html?refval=22%2F02352%2FFUL#documents_Sectio n (Accessed: 7 May 2023).

Business Live. (2022.). Huge Self-Storage Hub Planned for Bath. [Online] Available at: https://www.business-live.co.uk/commercial-property/huge-self-storage-hub-bath-24856065 (Accessed: 7 May 2023).

Control of Substances Hazardous to Health Regulations. (2002), SI 2002/2677. Available at: https://www.legislation.gov.uk/uksi/2002/2677/content s/made (Accessed: [Insert Date Accessed]).

Department for Business, Energy & Industrial Strategy.
(2021). The Non-Domestic Private Rented Sector
Minimum Energy Efficiency Standards:
Implementation of the EPC B Future Trajectory.
[Online] Available at:
https://assets.publishing.service.gov.uk/government/upl
oads/system/uploads/attachment_data/file/970192/non
-domestic-prs-mees-epc-b-future-trajectory-
implementation.pdf (Accessed: 7 May 2023).

Electricity at Work Regulations. (1989) SI 1989/635.
Available at:
https://www.legislation.gov.uk/uksi/1989/635/contents
/made (Accessed: 25th May 2023]).

Energy Advice Hub. (2023). Does Your Commercial
Building Meet the New Minimum Energy Efficiency
Standards? [Online] Available at:
https://energyadvicehub.org/does-your-commercial-
building-meet-the-new-minimum-energy-efficiency-
standards/ (Accessed: 7 May 2023).

GOV.UK. (2023). Non-domestic private rented
property minimum energy efficiency standard: landlord
guidance. [Online] Available at:
https://www.gov.uk/guidance/non-domestic-private-
rented-property-minimum-energy-efficiency-standard-
landlord-guidance (Accessed: 7 May 2023).

Gov.uk (2019) Guidance on PRS exemptions and Exemptions Register evidence requirements. Available at: https://www.gov.uk/government/publications/private-rented-sector-minimum-energy-efficiency-standard-exemptions/guidance-on-prs-exemptions-and-exemptions-register-evidence-requirements (Accessed: 21st May 2023).

Health and Safety at Work etc. Act 1974, c. 37. Available at: https://www.legislation.gov.uk/ukpga/1974/37/contents (Accessed: 25th May 2023).

Housing (Scotland) Act (2006) Section 14. Available at: https://www.legislation.gov.uk/asp/2006/1/section/14 (Accessed: 25th May 2023).

Knight Frank. (2023). Investment Yield Guide - May 2023. [Online] Available at: https://www.knightfrank.com/research/report-library/investment-yield-guide-may-2023-10140.aspx (Accessed: 7 May 2023).

Natasha Collins. (2017) The 1954 Act - Its importance in Commercial Property. [Online] available at: https://ncrealestate.co.uk/1954-act/ (accessed 29th May 2023).

Newark Works. (2022). About Newark Works. [Online] Available at: https://www.newarkworks.co.uk/about-newark-works/ (Accessed: 7 May 2023).

RICS (Royal Institution of Chartered Surveyors). (2022). RICS Valuation - Global Standards (The Red Book): Professional Standards. RICS.

RICS (Royal Institution of Chartered Surveyors). (2022). Code for Leasing Business Premises, 1st Edition. [Online]. Available at: https://www.rics.org/profession-standards/rics-standards-and-guidance/sector-standards/real-estate-standards/code-for-leasing-business-premises-1st-edition (Accessed: 9th June 2023).

Regulatory Reform (Fire Safety) Order (2005), SI 2005/1541. Available at: http://www.legislation.gov.uk/uksi/2005/1541/contents/made (Accessed: 21st May 2023).

Control of Asbestos Regulations. (2012) SI 2012/632. Available at: https://www.legislation.gov.uk/uksi/2012/632/contents/made (Accessed: [Insert Date Accessed]).

The Energy Efficiency (Private Rented Property) (England and Wales) Regulations (2015), SI 2015/962. Available at: https://www.legislation.gov.uk/uksi/2015/962/contents/made (Accessed: 21st May 2023).

The Gas Safety (Installation and Use) Regulations 1998, SI 1998/2451, as amended. Available at: https://www.legislation.gov.uk/uksi/1998/2451/contents/made (Accessed: 21st May 2023).

The Gas Safety (Installation and Use) Regulations 1998 (as amended) (Scotland), SSI 1998/187. Available at: https://www.legislation.gov.uk/ssi/1998/187/contents/made (Accessed: 21st May 2023).

Connect with Natasha

Listen to her podcast, *Honest Property Investment*, on iTunes, Spotify, Google Play, or on your favourite podcast app.

Read about the professional services she offers at ncrealestate.co.uk. Whilst you're on the website, make sure to sign up for the free resources which will also subscribe you to Natasha's weekly email list.

If you haven't yet, follow her on Instagram @ncrealestateltd.

And lastly, if you haven't managed to scan the QR code throughout the book to download the books resources, you can visit ncrealestate.co.uk/book to get access to all the resources mentioned throughout this book.

www.ingramcontent.com/pod-product-compliance
Lightning Source LLC
Chambersburg PA
CBHW071341210326
41597CB00015B/1521